P9-DDW-607

# COMMANDING

## YOUR

*Morning*

CINDY TRIMM

## Charisma
# HOUSE
### A STRANG COMPANY

MOST STRANG COMMUNICATIONS BOOK GROUP products are available at special quantity discounts for bulk purchase for sales promotions, premiums, fund-raising, and educational needs. For details, write Strang Communications Book Group, 600 Rinehart Road, Lake Mary, Florida 32746, or telephone (407) 333-0600.

COMMANDING YOUR MORNING by Cindy Trimm
Published by Charisma House
A Strang Company
600 Rinehart Road
Lake Mary, Florida 32746
www.strangbookgroup.com

This book or parts thereof may not be reproduced in any form, stored in a retrieval system, or transmitted in any form by any means—electronic, mechanical, photocopy, recording, or otherwise—without prior written permission of the publisher, except as provided by the United States of America copyright law.

Unless otherwise indicated, Scripture quotations are taken from the New King James Version of the Bible. Copyright © 1979, 1980, 1982 by Thomas Nelson, Inc. Used by permission. All rights reserved.

Scripture quotations marked AMP are from the Amplified Bible. Old Testament copyright © 1965, 1987 by the Zondervan Corporation. The Amplified New Testament copyright © 1954, 1958, 1987 by the Lockman Foundation. Used by permission.

Scripture quotations marked ESV are from The Holy Bible, English Standard Version. Copyright © 2001 by Crossway Bibles, a division of Good News Publishers. Used by permission. All rights reserved.

Scripture quotations marked KJV are taken from the King James Version of the Bible.

Scripture quotations marked NASU are from the New American Standard Bible—Updated Edition. Copyright © 1960, 1962, 1963, 1968, 1971, 1972, 1973, 1975, 1977, 1995 by The Lockman Foundation. Used by permission. (www.Lockman.org)

In her book *Commanding Your Morning*, Cindy Trimm has meticulously disclosed and unleashed the most awesome revelation of how to release the overcoming power that is in kingdom vision, and she has delivered insight to powerful and effective prayer and intercession. Her fresh, innovative, and masterful approach to any given subject matter, but especially this one, will leave you with an overwhelming and exciting expectancy. Cindy teaches us how to specifically decree and declare a thing and literally command our day. She has left no stone unturned, no holds barred, and no wondering how or why. This is the book that you will put right beside your Bible. It will enrich your life, day after blessed day. Since reading this book, I have experienced a paradigm shift in my life in the way I think, talk, live, pray, and believe. I have confidence that it will greatly impact your life as well.

—JUDY JACOBS
FOUNDER, HIS SONG MINISTRIES
HOST, *Judy Jacobs Now!*

Cindy Trimm in her book *Commanding Your Morning* clearly lays out biblical principles by which to govern your life. *Commanding Your Morning* gives you keys to walk in overcoming power in such a time as this. This book has been birthed out of the life of its author, Cindy Trimm. She is not a travel agent who is telling you about a beautiful place she has never been, but rather she is a tour guide who is telling you about where she has been.

Cindy Trimm is someone who is part of that remnant who has completely given her life for the building and establishing of God's kingdom. She has a deep compassion for people, a deep passion for the Lord, and a deep conviction for truth. Cindy Trimm, with a prophetic freshness and a keen biblical insight, will take you on a journey in *Commanding Your Morning* that will change your life. It is a must-read for every leader and believer in this day.

—Les Bowling, President and Founder
Eagle Rock Church and Eagle Rock
Covenant Network

As an author, I read many books to gain perspective and instruction over what I am attempting to communicate. On occasion I find a book that makes me say to myself, "This captures my heart. I have never read nor could I have communicated this principle so well. This is a jewel in my hand!"

*Commanding Your Morning* by Cindy Trimm is such a book! My life message is restoration through meditation. *Commanding Your Morning* both disciplines, transforms, and unlocks your mind while you read. This is a book of action! You will find the Lord's thoughts forming and your thought processes realigning. Then you will experience your mouth being filled with decrees that will determine your future success in life! If I could choose one book to go with His Book, that one book would be *Commanding Your Morning*!

—Chuck Pierce, President
Glory of Zion International Ministries

Scripture quotations marked NIV are from the Holy Bible, New International Version. Copyright © 1973, 1978, 1984, International Bible Society. Used by permission.

Scripture quotations marked NLT are from the Holy Bible, New Living Translation. Copyright © 1996, 2004. Used by permission of Tyndale House Publishers, Inc., Wheaton, IL 60189. All rights reserved.

Scripture quotations marked NLV are from The Holy Bible, New Life Version. Copyright © 1969 by Christian Literature International. Used by permission. All rights reserved.

Scripture quotations marked THE MESSAGE are from *The Message: The Bible in Contemporary English*. Copyright © 1993, 1994, 1995, 1996, 2000, 2001, 2002. Used by permission of NavPress Publishing Group.

Design Director: Bill Johnson
Cover design by The DesignWorks Group, Tim Green
              www.thedesignworks.com
Author photos by: Reggie Anderson Photography,
              www.reggiephotos4u.com

Copyright © 2007 by Cindy Trimm
All rights reserved

Library of Congress Cataloging-in-Publication Data

Trimm, N. Cindy.
  Commanding your morning / by N. Cindy Trimm.
     p. cm.
  ISBN 978-1-59979-177-7
  1. Prayer--Christianity. 2. Spiritual warfare. I. Title.
  BV210.3.T75 2007
  248.4--dc22

                                        2007023882

09 10 11 12 13 — 11 10 9 8 7 6 5

Printed in the United States of America

**This book is dedicated to my family:**

My mother, Edna Trimm, whose unconditional love, guidance, and mentorship have been the wind beneath my wings.

And to my siblings Charlene, Marilyn, Winston, Deborah, and Freda, whose passion for life and unwavering support have awarded you all premier places within my relational constellation. Did you know that you are my heroes and she-roes? I could think of no greater family than mine to have been honored by God to be a part of.

## ACKNOWLEDGMENTS

Divine inspiration transforms good works into master-pieces. I acknowledge that God alone gets the glory for this divinely inspired work. To my staff both past and present: you, who over the years bowed low in servanthood and sacrifice so that I could think, develop, and create. I could never speak of success and not acknowledge that all great men and women are great because of the greatness of those who serve them. I am forever grateful to you and will forever hold you close to my heart and uplift you in my prayers. I also thank those who make up an invaluable and inspirational team at Strang Communications. May God forever favor you. Also, to Embassy Center of Empowerment, you mean the world to me.

# CONTENTS

# FOREWORD

*T*HERE IS NO ACTIVITY ON EARTH MORE COMMON THAN prayer. Every culture does it. Every race does it. Every religion does it. However, there is no more frustrating, confusing, and suspicious area of human experience than prayer. There are more questions surrounding this religious activity than any other in every generation. Does it really work? Does God answer prayer? Does prayer make a difference? Can prayer affect circumstances? Why does it seem that some prayers are answered and others are not? Why should we pray? The questions go on and on.

My own personal experience was plagued with such questions and provided adequate cause for doubt and suspicion regarding the subject of prayer. Over the years my studies and research took me to explore many of the great writers on the subject, and today I am pleased to testify that my experience in prayer has been one of daily improvement and success.

When I was asked to review this work by Cindy Trimm, I was excited, knowing that her commitment to excellence in anything she approaches would yield an outstanding contribution to this subject of prayer and intercession. I was not disappointed.

*Commanding Your Morning* is destined to be a classic as it simplifies but does not dilute the gravity of this very critical human spiritual activity. Cindy, with her skillful use of language, leaps over complicated theological jargon and delivers principles that make the daily exercise of prayer embracing and attractive. I challenge those who are disappointed with their prayer lives, the scholar who dares to think beyond the known, and the student of Scripture who desires to know more about prayers as a dominant force in the earthly enforcement of the heavenly kingdom to read this book.

*Commanding Your Morning* releases the overcoming power in the hearts of those who read, receive, and apply these instructions in their daily lives. I firmly believe the precepts in this book will enhance your encounter with the kingdom in the area of strategic prayer and intercession. The revolutionary approach to prayer inside this book will reinforce and welcome deeper revelatory truths on this subject. It is with this confidence that I challenge you, the reader, to peel from every page the treasure house of wisdom buried within each sentence and experience your ability to command the morning.

The Word of God revealed through these pages has the ability to realign that which is misaligned, including mind-sets, belief systems, ideologies, traditions, and doctrines of deception that exalt themselves above the will of God in the lives of His people. *Commanding Your Morning* instructs the believer on how to pull down these strongholds and bring them into captivity under the lordship of Christ.

I highly commend Cindy Trimm for this vital contribution to the world of faith, and I hope millions will benefit from its time-tested eternal truths.

—Dr. Myles Munroe
President, BFM/ITWLA International
Nassau, Bahamas

# INTRODUCTION

Only as high as I reach can I grow, only as far as I
seek can I go, only as deep as I look can I see, only
as much as I dream can I be.[1]
—Karen Ravn

AVE YOU EVER HAD THE GNAWING FEELING ON
the inside that you were not getting everything
you were supposed to get out of life—a feeling that life
was full of possibilities, but somehow you could never
figure out how to tap into them? Have you ever looked at
another person's life, marriage, financial status, or career
and wondered, "What's wrong with me?" Well, you are
not alone.

Many people have come to believe that life is a mystery
that cannot be solved. They think that success and prosperity are destined for everyone except them, and they
feel powerless and victimized as the events of their lives
spiral out of control. They would do something about it
if they knew what to do, but the truth of the matter is
that they have tried everything they know and come up
empty every time. What they need is a new set of keys

to unlock all that God is holding for them in their lives. This book is about the keys that will help you escape these "prisons of the mind."

Still, there are others who may experience short seasons of success but then despairingly long seasons of trials, tribulation, setbacks, and lack. Their lives are governed by success-undermining maxims such as: "Stuff happens," "Life is unpredictable," "All good things must come to an end," "If it is not one thing, it's another," and "This is as good as it gets." These folks are ignorant of the fact that they are victims of their own self-fulfilling prophecies.

What neither of these groups understands is that we define our lives by our every thought and word. If we want our lives to change, it all starts with what we think and say.

This is precisely why Proverbs 23:7 tells us, "For as he [a man or woman] thinks in his heart, so is he."

You must realize that the Word of God has the power to realign anything that is misaligned, especially faulty mind-sets, belief systems, ideologies, traditions, and doctrines of deception that lie and exalt themselves above the will of God for your life. Life does not have to be a mystery for you. You do not have to continue mindlessly groping in the dark for the right path through life. God already has your success, prosperity, and fulfillment all planned out; you just have to follow His directions to find it. As the Scriptures say:

> For I know the thoughts that I think toward you, says the LORD, thoughts of peace and not of evil, to give you a future and a hope.
> —Jeremiah 29:11

You can take control of your life and experience divine success and prosperity by following God's directions outlined in His Word. He has a wonderful plan for you—and His plan for your personal world depends on you fulfilling it by first taking control of your mind and your mouth. Learn to fill your thoughts and words with light and truth. Amen

The Bible specifically tells us that we can reside in the best of two possible worlds—a spiritual realm characterized by happiness, empowered living, success, and prosperity. Through a relationship with God we are miraculously conveyed into the kingdom of light—a realm that opens unlimited doors of opportunity, enabling us to discover our divine purpose, maximize our best potential, and experience boundless abundance. Light is not only the absence of darkness, but it is also the yoke-breaking presence of God, the liberating essence of truth, and the mind-transforming potential of every revelation of God— it is all that is good within and among us. All good things find their beginning in Him, and without Him nothing good exists.

Every new day with God brings the dawn of new and better possibilities. Today could turn out to be the best day of your life—but how it ends largely depends on how you begin it. You are in charge of taking control of your day from its very beginning—something I call "commanding your morning"—and as you do, know that whatever begins with God has to end right. My prayer for you is that as you read the following pages, God will reveal the power within you—and that your hope of glory would be made more real as you learn to command your morning through the wisdom of His truth every single day.

No matter how good or bad your life is, every circumstance can change for the best if you learn how to command your morning before your day begins.

## CHAPTER ONE

# THE SECRET IS OUT

The workings of the human heart are the profoundest mystery of the universe. One moment they make us despair of our kind, and the next we see in them the reflection of the divine image.[1]

—Charles W. Chesnutt

ONE OF THE FASTEST-GROWING ART FORMS TODAY IS called the "spoken word." Throngs of people gather in clubs, schools, cafés, church auditoriums, stadiums, and theaters just to hear the poetic, pulsating rhyme spoken by artists who by virtue of their creativity and talent move their audiences to emotional highs and lows merely by what comes out of their mouths. Like painters creating moving masterpieces in vibrant colors, these artists "paint" on the canvas of the human soul.

Eons ago, with neither fanfare nor audience, the mighty Creator of the universe spoke. His utterance would constitute the first recorded words, "Let there be…" (See Genesis 1.) God thought, spoke, and the universe came into being.

The true power of the spoken word is beyond our

common understanding. It is a spiritual mystery—a hidden secret now being revealed to equip God's people for an unprecedented era of empowerment and influence. The time has come for believers to rise up and walk in the knowledge and authority God has provided and commanded through His Word—the Word He spoke into us and created us to speak forth. While forces around us threaten our peace and stability, nothing can prevail against God's spoken Word. Amen.

## THE GREAT POWER OF SMALL THINGS

Everything in the universe begins with and revolves around two things: *words* and *thoughts*. These two elements form the creative substance that molds and shapes the destiny of humanity. Each of us becomes the person we are, chooses the direction we take, and accomplishes everything we do based on these two primary elements.

> **Everything in the universe begins with and revolves around two things: *words* and *thoughts*.**

Our thoughts, intentions, motivations, and aspirations—whether they be secretly pondered in the heart, openly declared as desires, or formally written as goals—mold and shape our personal universe into something that is either grand and beautiful or base and hideous. Whatever you harbor in the innermost corridors of your thought life will, sooner or later, reveal itself in the outer arena through your words or actions. Whatever is hidden will eventually be brought to light. First Corinthians 4:5 tells us God "will bring to light the things now hidden in darkness and will disclose the purposes of the heart" (ESV). Just as a seed is for a time hidden under the ground, it will eventually break through the surface and its true essence will be revealed.

Just as in every seed, there is life-giving power that resides in every spoken word. This principle illustrates how the spiritual law of incubation and manifestation works. Everything you see in the natural began as a spiritual seed—that is, as a thought.

The temporal realm has its roots in the spiritual. Grabbing hold of this profound spiritual truth will enable you to make critical connections that can transform your life. Once you understand that the spiritual realm is the "causal realm," you will begin to grasp the massive power of your thoughts, ideas, words, and prayers—spiritual things that engineer, mold, and craft the current and future state of your temporal existence.

We are told in 2 Peter 1:3–4 that God, in His infinite wisdom, has already given us all things pertaining to life (the Wycliffe version says, "all things of his god-like virtue") that we might partake of His divine nature. Included in this celestial equipping are divine thoughts and inspired words. As a spiritual being created in the image of God (Gen. 1:26), your spiritual genes hold the creative power to frame your personal world by the thoughts and words you think and speak, which are divine tools given for your creative use. All you are, experience, and ultimately achieve can be traced back to how you have made use of these two simple, yet vastly powerful, tools—your words and thoughts.

## ONE OF LIFE'S GREATEST MYSTERIES

The power of the spoken word is one of life's greatest mysteries. All that you will ever be or accomplish hinges on how you choose to govern what comes out of your mouth. By what you allow to occupy your mind and mouth, you can either bless your life to great heights of success or send it orbiting into realms of failure, sadness, and discontentment. This is why Proverbs tells us, "For as he thinks in his heart, so is he" (Prov. 23:7, AMP), and urges, "Guard your heart above all else, for it determines the course of your life" (Prov. 4:23, NLT). Jesus followed suit by declaring, "For whatever is in your heart determines what you say. A good person produces good things from the treasury of a good heart, and an evil person produces evil things from the treasury of an evil heart" (Matt. 12:34–35, NLT).

What occupies your mind determines what eventually

> All you are, experience, and ultimately achieve can be traced back to how you have made use of these two simple, yet vastly powerful, tools—your words and thoughts.

fills your mouth; your outer world showcases all that has dominated—and at times subjugated—your inner world. Because the law of cause and effect is continually at work, there is always an inner cause for every outer effect. Your outer world is a direct result of your inner world. Every circumstance in life is a result of a choice—and every choice is the result of a thought. All those things that fill your mind hold the keys to your reality. Your thoughts provide the fuel for your words, and your words provide the fuel for your world.

It is therefore imperative that you understand the nature of what you are saying. Are you aware of the true meaning of the things you are speaking out? We would do well to heed the advice of one ancient Stoic philosopher named Epictetus who once said: "First learn the meaning of what you say, and then speak."

Hosea, the prophetic sage of old, remarked, "For they sow the wind, and they shall reap the whirlwind" (Hosea 8:7, ESV). In other words, each one of us must take responsibility for what we experience in life. We are the sum total of every choice that we have ever made or let happen. If you do not like where you are, you are only one thought away from turning toward the life you desire. Amen

If this is to happen, it is paramount that you become the master of your thoughts. Sift your thought life. Filter out anything that you do not want to show up in your future, and focus on what you truly desire. God wired your thoughts to have power so you would be equipped to overcome every obstacle. He fashioned you to create, innovate, strategize, and succeed—

**It is paramount that you become the master of your thoughts.**

and just to be sure, He put His own divine thoughts and nature within you. As God says in Jeremiah 31:33, "I will put my instructions deep within them, and I will write them on their hearts" (NLT).

Hook up your heart with the ultimate power source.

## WHAT'S YOUR FREQUENCY?

The law of cause and effect also works with the law of attraction. Simply put, this means "like attracts like." If thoughts are things and things are made up of substance, then the material manifested in our lives is attracted to us by our spiritual thoughts. In other words, inspired experiences are caused by inspired thoughts.

I know a woman who is brilliantly gifted. Over the years I have observed the great people who have come into her life and the great things that have happened to her, time and time again. But for absolutely no apparent reason, every success would only last a short while before ending dismally. It was quite a challenge to convince her that the problem was not with other people or external circumstances. After months of persistent coaching, she informed me one day with great excitement that, finally, good people and circumstances had come to stay. The secret was simple. She changed the spirit of her thoughts and words. As long as she aligned her thoughts and speech with doubtful, negative beliefs, that is exactly what she experienced, but once she aligned herself with hopeful, optimistic beliefs, her world changed accordingly.

Your thoughts and words are transmitted like a shortwave radio signal. They send messages out on a specific frequency and are transmitted back to you manifested as an experience or occurrence in your life. Your thoughts create something like a magnetic field around you, while your words provide a kind of spiritual homing device that attract either positive people, things, and experiences or negative people, things, and experiences.

Therefore, you must learn to fill your mind with good, godly, and great thoughts. As we are told in Philippians 4:8, you must "fix your thoughts on what is true, and honorable, and right, and pure, and lovely, and admirable. Think about things that are excellent and worthy of praise" (NLT). What you think has the power to literally transform your life.

It is essential that you become extremely vigilant about what enters your mind daily. What you hear affects how you think and what you believe. The prophet Isaiah had insight into how important it is to heed what you say, hear, and see when he declared:

He who walks righteously and speaks uprightly...
who stops his ears from hearing of bloodshed
and shuts his eyes from looking on evil,
he will dwell on the heights;
his place of defense will be the fortresses of rocks;
his bread will be given him; his water will be sure.
—Isaiah 33:15–16, ESV

If you want to have life-affirming thoughts—thoughts of success and prosperity—then fill your ears with words that will produce these things in your life. Eventually, if you hear something enough, over time it will form a belief, and that belief will produce a corresponding action. It is this hearing—and hearing again—that is the impetus of faith. As the apostle Paul said, "So faith comes from hearing, and hearing through the word of Christ" (Rom. 10:17, ESV). In other words, it comes from "hearing and hearing." Make sure you are grounding your beliefs and basing your faith on God's "rich life"—not some counterfeit, but the abundance of His kingdom—by filling your heart and mind with life-giving, biblical truth.

Jesus Christ, a kingdom-practitioner, knew the power of truth combined with the principle of faith. He knew that faith came by hearing. So, He spent hours teaching and dialoguing with His disciples. He taught His students success principles derived from spiritual laws in order to build their faith in their ability to make a difference in the world. He began the arduous task of transforming the mind-sets of twelve outcasts and fishermen. He spoke many spiritual truths to them in order to stretch their spiritual paradigms of success and prosperity beyond the temporal, three-dimensional realm. He knew it would take constant exposure to the Light for the light to finally turn on in them.

## LET THERE BE LIGHT

Sometimes when concepts are difficult for you to grasp or comprehend, you simply need to say, "Let there be light!" The first recorded thing God said was, "Let there be light." Light illuminates. What you really want is for your spirit and your mind to be illuminated—you want to obtain insight and wisdom. When it feels as if you are wandering in the dark and can't figure out what to do, stop and command, "Let there be light!" Amen

A minister friend was having difficulty paying the bills of her ministry. It had become an almost insurmount-able task. When one bill was paid, there were several left unpaid. The bills kept coming without sufficient income to cover them, until one day she began uttering four simple words, "Let there be light."

She stopped focusing on her difficulty and started focusing on the answer: God's light. She let the light of His goodness fill her mind and, following her heavenly Father's example, commanded that light be made manifest by the words of her mouth. The answer had always been there, but it had been hidden from her conscious mind because her focus on the problem prohibited her from seeing the solution. In a way, when she finally saw the light, there was light. God revealed innovative ways for her to not only pay the bills but also to prosper. She now has a thriving ministry and a million-dollar business.

Four simple words opened her spirit to receive divine wisdom from God. These four simple words can help you, too. Don't hesitate to speak out in faith, "Let there be light!" Speak these words over perplexing situations and watch God work. Remember, "Every good gift and every perfect gift is from above, and comes down from the Father of lights, with whom there is no variation or shadow of turning" (James 1:17). God wants you to have what is good and perfect. Did you get that? You don't just have to have good health; you can have perfect health. You don't have to settle for a good job; you can have a perfect job, or better still, the perfect business that not only pays the bills but also gives you enough left over to be a tremendous blessing to others. You don't have to settle for a good marriage; you can have the perfect marriage. You don't have to settle for a good life; you can have a perfect life. So go ahead; shout it from the rooftops, "Let there be light!" You will be delightfully surprised that perhaps what you have been looking for is right before your eyes. It was simply awaiting illumination.

Jesus wanted the light to come on for His disciples. To

teach complex spiritual principles He would use simple stories based on common subjects. Jesus would weave revolutionary spiritual truths into the fabric of each parable. After one famous allegory referring to how seed is sown in various soils, His disciples asked Him, "Why do you speak to the people in parables?" He replied:

> The knowledge of the secrets of the kingdom of heaven has been given to you, but not to them. Whoever has will be given more, and he will have an abundance. Whoever does not have, even what he has will be taken from him. This is why I speak to them in parables.
> —Matthew 13:10–13, NIV

Did you get that? As long as information remains a secret, hidden in obscurity, no one can prosper from it, no matter how powerful the secret or how mighty the person. But that person to whom it is made known, no matter who, will have access to abundance; to whom it is not revealed, even that which this person has shall be taken away.

This is a powerful passage of Scripture. Not only does Jesus tell a powerful parable here, but also, sandwiched between the initial telling of it in verses 1–9 and His explanation of its meaning in verses 18–23, Jesus takes a moment to clarify why He is using parables to teach in the first place. The rationale He offers for His method is as illuminating as the parable itself:

Though seeing, they do not see; though hearing, they do not hear or understand. In them is fulfilled the prophecy of Isaiah: "You will be ever hearing but never understanding; you will be ever seeing but never perceiving. For this people's heart has become calloused; they hardly hear with their ears, and they have closed their eyes. Otherwise they might see with their eyes, hear with their ears, understand with their hearts and turn, and I would heal them."

But blessed are your eyes because they see, and your ears because they hear. For I tell you the truth, many prophets and righteous men longed to see what you see but did not see it, and to hear what you hear but did not hear it.

—Matthew 13:13–17, NIV

The importance and power of understanding are not only the reasons for His method of teaching, but they are also the very point of the lesson itself. At the crux of it all is the divine power of revelation—truly seeing, or grasping, spiritual truth. When men "see the light" they will come to the knowledge of the truth and experience abundant life. John phrased it this way: "In him was life, and that life was the light of men. The light shines in the darkness, but the darkness has not understood it" (John 1:4–5, NIV). John referred to Jesus as "the true light that gives light to every man" (v. 9, NIV). It is Jesus who not only gives us light but also gives the ability to "see the light." In his letter to the Corinthians, Paul wrote, "For God, who said, 'Let light shine out of darkness,' made his light shine in our hearts to give us the light of the knowledge of the glory of God in the face of Christ" (2 Cor. 4:6, NIV).

In the parable about the seed (truth or light) and the soil (our hearts), Jesus spoke in such a way as to reveal the secret to success and prosperity. He is speaking about understanding—about "possessing light." Let's look at how He explains the meaning further down in the chapter:

> Listen then to what the parable of the sower means: When anyone hears the message about the kingdom and does not understand it, the evil one comes and snatches away what was sown in his heart.... But the one who received the seed that fell on good soil is the man who hears the word and understands it. He produces a crop, yielding a hundred, sixty or thirty times what was sown.
> —Matthew 13:18–19, 23, NIV

Jesus is talking about our ability to understand—He is addressing the issue of the state of a man's mind. Out of our mind we produce a crop based on what we have sown in understanding—based on what we have understood. David cried out "to him who by understanding made the heavens" (Ps. 136:5, ESV) and "[gave] me understanding that

I may live" (Ps. 119:144, ESV). In Proverbs we read, "Understanding will guard you" (Prov. 2:11, ESV) and "Blessed is the one…who gets understanding" (Prov. 3:13, ESV).

Above all else, seek understanding. "Gird up the loins of your mind" (1 Pet. 1:13) by pursuing knowledge, wisdom, and truth—and out of that abundance your mouth will speak words that will frame your world. Make it a habit to examine what your thoughts are chasing after and what your words are gathering to you. Remember, the world within not only colors the world without, but it is also its blueprint. Be intentional in what you hear, how you think, and what you speak—for you are setting the stage for the reality you experience.

> Walk while you have the light, lest darkness overtake you. The one who walks in the darkness does not know where he is going. While you have the light, believe in the light, that you may become sons of light. Amen
>
> —John 12:35–36, ESV

## UNLOCK THE MYSTERY

Everyone loves to be in on a secret. One of the worst things is feeling left out when it comes to being "in the know"—as if everyone is aware of something vitally important except for you. But worse than that is the feeling there are important things everyone should know but few do. The Bible calls these types of secrets *mysteries.* For most people, life is exactly that, a mystery. But Jesus came to help us solve our mysteries. He came to give us knowledge of the truth.

The key to victory in Christ—and in this life—is the knowledge and wisdom that unlocks the mysteries of life. That is why God wants you to pursue wisdom and understanding above all else.

> Get wisdom! Get understanding!
> Do not forget, nor turn away from the words of
>     my mouth....
> Wisdom is the principal thing;
> Therefore get wisdom.
> And in all your getting, get understanding.
> —Proverbs 4:5, 7

Seek to know and understand how and why God has created you. This is one secret you can be in on! There is overcoming power in knowing it is God's desire for you to succeed and prosper, as well as knowing how He has designed you to create success and abundance in every sphere you influence.

When I say "abundance," I am not talking about materialism or consumerism. What I am talking about is the fact that it is God's will for you to live without lack—to provide you with every possible thing you need to successfully fulfill your purpose and maximize your potential. This certainly includes material things, but more importantly it means

Spirit-inspired thoughts, declarations, and conversations; divinely appointed relationships, business opportunities, and challenges—and above all else, supernatural gifts and abilities as you acknowledge every good thing that is in you in Christ. (See Philemon 6.)

> There is overcoming power in knowing it is God's desire for you to succeed and prosper, as well as knowing how He has designed you to create success and abundance in every sphere you influence.

I appreciate the story of Dave Thomas, founder of Wendy's, who was raised by adoptive parents. As a child, Dave always imagined one day owning a hamburger restaurant, and on November 15, 1969, the first Wendy's Old Fashioned Hamburgers opened.[2] Dave Thomas personifies that if you can see it in your mind first, you can achieve it. Yes

So, my friend, the secret is out. It is your time to consciously paint the canvas of your life with whatever you aspire to achieve. Fill your mind with majestic thoughts. Generate excitement and expectation with every word that proceeds from your mouth. I urge you to create a master-piece out of your life. Dare to imagine!

## CHAPTER TWO

# MIND YOUR OWN BUSINESS

Our life is what our thoughts make it.[1]

—Marcus Aurelius

[A man] will find that as he alters his thoughts toward things, and other people, things and other people will alter towards him.[2]

—James Allen

YOU MUST LEARN TO HARNESS THE POWER OF YOUR thoughts if you are to effectively reign as a king and priest on this earth. You must understand who you were created to be. You are a child of God and His representative in the earth. As such, He has given you power, authority, and dominion to overcome adversities and all of your adversaries. You are told in Ephesians 6:12 that your fight is not with flesh and blood but with powers and principalities. This fight can't be won with your hands but only with your mind and mouth.

> For our struggle is not against flesh and blood, but against the rulers, against the authorities,

against the powers of this dark world and against the spiritual forces of evil in the heavenly realms. Therefore put on the full armor of God, so that when the day of evil comes, you may be able to stand your ground, and after you have done every-thing, to stand.

—Ephesians 6:12–13, NIV

You must become as skilled in your thoughts and speech as a swordsman is with his sword. Taking control of your thoughts will cause you to gain control over your life. That is what putting on the armor of God is all about. Amen

## POSSESSING THE LAND

The first thing you must do in taking possession of all God has prepared for you is to take possession of your thoughts.

**We must understand who we were created to be as children of God, and we must understand the authority we have in Christ.**

You may not think this requires a great deal of effort, let alone training or practice, but there is only one thing harder to master than your thoughts, and that is your tongue! (See James 3:8.) Winning the battle in your thought life requires meditating daily on the truths found in Scripture, studying diligently to show yourself approved, and becoming an earnest and lifelong student of the art of spiritual warfare.

Throughout the New Testament we are told that our battles do not take place in the temporal realm but in the spiritual realm. In nearly every book of the New Testament, we are told to "not be afraid; only believe" (Mark 5:36), "gird up the loins of your mind" (1 Pet. 1:3), "renew your mind" (Rom. 12:2), and put on "the mind of Christ" (1 Cor. 2:16). We are taught in Romans that "to set the mind on the flesh is death, but to set the mind on the Spirit is life and peace" (Rom. 8:6, ESV). We are instructed to take every thought captive:

> For the weapons of our warfare are not of the flesh but have divine power to destroy strongholds. We destroy arguments and every lofty opinion raised against the knowledge of God, and take every thought captive to obey Christ.
> —2 Corinthians 10:4–5, ESV

Every battle is won or lost in the arena of your mind. One of the most heartbreaking stories of the Old Testament is told in Numbers when the Israelites disobeyed God by refusing to take possession of the land He had prepared for them. Because they saw themselves as small and weak—they believed in their own minds that they were as grasshoppers before giants—they were unable to fulfill God's call. The giants, who themselves had been afraid of the children of Israel, were instead empowered because of the Israelites' fear. "We seemed to ourselves like grasshoppers, and so we seemed to them" (Num. 13:33, ESV).

It was fear alone that caused the Israelites to miss out on the promise of God. Instead of inheriting property, they were forced to wander homeless until the next generation rose up bold enough to take possession and move in. Among those allowed to become property owners were Joshua and Caleb, the only two of the former generation given the right to hold title and deed in the land of promise. It is recorded in Numbers 13:30 that when the Israelites cried out in fear before Moses, it was Caleb who spoke up, saying, "Let's go at once to take the land. We can certainly conquer it!" God honored Caleb's faith.

But what compelled Caleb to speak with such boldness? What was it about Joshua and Caleb that set them apart? The secret to their success is summed up in the first chapter of Joshua. God gave very specific instructions to Joshua about how to secure success, prosperity, and victory over every adversary:

> This Book of the Law shall not depart from your mouth, but you shall meditate in it day and night, that you may observe to do according to all that is written in it. For then you will make your way prosperous, and then you will have good success. Have I not commanded you? Be strong and of good

courage; do not be afraid, nor be dismayed, for the
LORD your God is with you wherever you go.
—Joshua 1:8–9

God instructed Joshua to meditate on His Word day and night so that it would fill his heart, mind, and mouth. Then He commanded him to be strong and courageous. Do you see the connection? Until his mind and mouth only thought and spoke God's Word, Joshua could not have any hope of being strong and of good courage. Right from the outset God made it a priority to address the issue of Joshua's mind—no other instructions or strategies took precedence over what occupied Joshua's thoughts.

## AS A MAN THINKETH

You are the sum total of your thoughts. I have learned that as your deepest driving desire is, so is your will; as your will is, so are your deeds; as your deeds are, so is your destiny. Just as it was important for Joshua to govern his thoughts by the Word of the Lord, it is important for you to meditate daily on God's Word—allowing it to fill your mind before anything else. But you have it better today because Jesus has come. You have the Word made flesh—the Spirit of Christ—residing in you. You have been given the name above every name as your spiritual authority, and you have a two-edged sword, which is the Word of God, at your disposal. Do you see how important God's Word is?

All things are possible to those who believe (Mark 9:23), but without knowledge of the Word, you don't have the correct truths to believe.

As you follow God's specific instructions and fill your thoughts with those things the Bible tells you to, you will discover that the world will begin to unfold before you with an array of possibilities and reflect back what you choose to focus upon. It is critically important to stay conscious of what's going on in your mind. Random thoughts lead to random accomplishments that rarely build upon one another. Look at how Paul puts it in Philippians:

> Summing it all up, friends, I'd say you'll do best by filling your minds and meditating on things true, noble, reputable, authentic, compelling, gracious— the best, not the worst; the beautiful, not the ugly; things to praise, not things to curse....Do that, and God, who makes everything work together, will work you into his most excellent harmonies.
> —Philippians 4:8–9, THE MESSAGE

Look at what Paul again says in Romans:

> Do not be conformed to this world, but be transformed by the renewing of your mind, so that you may prove what the will of God is, that which is good and acceptable and perfect.
> —Romans 12:2, NASU

How do you renew your mind? Through knowledge of the truth regarding who you are in Christ. If you were to build your life like a house of faith, knowledge of God would be its foundation, while knowledge of who you are in Christ would be its frame. From the Bible, two things we know about faith are: (1) it is impossible to please God without it (Heb. 11:6), and (2) in the words of Jesus, "It shall be done to you according to your faith" (Matt. 9:29, NASU). If you do not take control of your inner thoughts, you will become a slave to your outer circumstances. You won't be driving your life; the storms and changing weather will.

Don't be left out in the dark as an exile estranged from the good life God has for you. Paul wrote, "They are darkened in their understanding, alienated from the life of God because of the ignorance that is in them" (Eph. 4:18, ESV). Do not be among those who perish for lack of knowledge. (See Hosea 4:6.) Be "in the know," unlock God's secrets for you, and get in on the good life.

## THE ORIGIN OF INSPIRATION

Eighteenth-century poet and theologian Johann Gottfried Von Herder has been quoted as saying, "Without inspiration the best powers of the mind remain dormant; there is a fuel within us which needs to be ignited with sparks."[3]

Thoughts are spiritual, and so is the inspirational process. Man begins with a concept in his mind, something he believes he is able to accomplish; he joins his will and intellect to his imagination; and then expectation sees it through. In Genesis 11, the people thought to themselves that they could build a tower to heaven, and because they saw this tower in their minds, they were able to build it. God stopped them by causing confusion and making it impossible for them to communicate, because the tower became an idol for them. However, this story still illustrates the power of our thoughts and words.

> And the Lord said, Behold, they are one people and they have all one language; and this is only the beginning of what they will do, and now nothing they have imagined they can do will be impossible for them.
>
> —Genesis 11:6, AMP

## THINK—FOR A CHANGE

Every circumstance in your life can be changed for the best. The moment you convert your imagination into intentions and your intentions into actions, a change must occur. A profound example of someone who changed his humble circumstances by means of the power of thinking is the composer extraordinaire and music impresario Quincy Jones. In his words, he was inspired by every band that came through town. He had no training at all, but he was fueled by inspiration to learn from every opportunity available. He was known to call on Ray Charles in the early hours of the morning whenever he came to town. He was practically adopted by Count Basie at the age of thirteen. As soon as Quincy picked up the trumpet, he heard arrangements of ensembles in his head, and his reputation as an arranger grew.[4] He is the all-time most-nominated Grammy artist with a total of seventy-nine Grammy nominations.[5] Quincy Jones was inspired.

George Washington Carver was inspired to grow and produce peanuts. Starting out as a farmhand, Carver later attended Tuskegee University and revolutionized the southern agricultural economy by thinking up more than two hundred products that could be derived from the peanut and more than one hundred different products that could be derived from the sweet potato. These products included soap, ink, plastics, axle grease, flour, molasses, vinegar, and rubber, just to name a few.[6]

Imagination is the natural product of meditation. Life's opportunities and creativity diminish or explode based on your ability to harness your imagination. Albert Einstein said, "I am enough of an artist to draw freely upon my imagination. Imagination is more important than knowledge. Knowledge is limited. Imagination encircles the world."[7] If we can think of imagination as a door that opens to a world of possibilities, then intentions and the corresponding actions are the keys that unlock that door.

Einstein was considered a slow learner, possibly due to

dyslexia. Yet he imagined, postulated, and propelled the theory of relativity to the forefront of modern science, winning the 1921 Nobel Prize in Physics.[8] What we know of quantum physics can largely be attributed to the contributions of Albert Einstein. More than any other, this field of science has confirmed biblical truth about the relationship between faith and the "miraculous." Both testify to the truth that whatever can be imagined already exists; it simply exists in another dimension—in another form or substance—and this is the source of all inspiration.

Accordingly, God conceived and by His Spirit spoke into existence all that is. He brought what already existed in the spiritual into the temporal by the power of His Word. He breathed that creative force—His very Spirit—into humanity. It is His Spirit in you that gives inspiration and understanding of what already exists in the spiritual realm. There is a "spirit in man, the breath of the Almighty, that makes him understand" (Job 32:8, ESV). That spirit in you has always existed—it is eternal—and it is the source of all revelation and inspiration.

God's Spirit creates a blueprint in the form of understanding, and from that blueprint all things come to be. Before we had the computer, certain people saw a necessity for it and were inspired. This inspiration came out of the realm of the spirit. From the computer to symphonies to cures for cancer, everything started as an inspiration. All good inspiration comes from God. He is the Great

Inspirer and the Almighty Enabler. All things are possible to those who put their trust in Him. (See Mark 10:27.) Amen

Inspiration is a God thing. Inspiration is God Himself speaking into the human spirit. Inspirational thoughts are God finding expression for His will through the minds of human beings. According to Jeremiah 29:11, God's thoughts are good and not evil. I want to remind you that God is up to something good, and He has you in mind—above and beyond what you could ask or imagine! (See Ephesians 3:20.) Amen Let it be

The great "imagineer," Walt Disney, exemplified this principle. Not only was he able to tap into the power of imagination, but also what he brought forth was pure goodness and joy transforming the world of family entertainment. He was known as a pioneer and innovator and the "possessor of one of the most fertile and unique imaginations the world has ever known."[9] Who would ever think that a mouse, a duck, and a storybook fairy could prove such a force in the world's powerful entertainment industry? Disney had the ability to see beyond the status quo into the realm of limitless possibilities, interweaving technology, engineering, art, and imagination in unprecedented ways. His imagination propelled him into the future and brought into existence new forms of art and entertainment never before thought possible. Today we have Disneyland and Disney World, the world's greatest theme parks, because of the seed planted by the imagination of just this one man.

Our lives are built by a series of thoughts, much as bricks are used to build a house. The bricks are what bring it forth from a piece of paper and make it three-dimensional. As a man thinks in his heart—in the present active continuum, as he continues to think—he is building his life one brick at a time.

Your every present thought is a significant building block in determining the quality of your future. Many of us build lives like shanties, while others build mansions. If your thoughts are inferior, your life will be inferior; but if your thoughts are lofty and honorable, you are laying the foundation to live accordingly.

## ENLARGE YOUR TERRITORY

There is a direct correlation between the quality of your thoughts and the quality of your life. What you think determines who you are; it determines what you are, where you go, what you acquire, where you live, whom you love, where you work, what you accomplish, what you read—I could go on and on. James Allen wrote in his timeless classic *As a Man Thinketh*, "All that a man achieves and all that he fails to achieve is the direct result of his own thoughts."[10] If your life is going to change, you must think for a change. You are always only one thought away from changing your life. As Joel Osteen says, you can live your best life now!

Virginia can live your best life now
Let it be!

Here's the principle: you will never have more or go further or accomplish greater things than your thoughts will allow you. Therefore, you must create an opulent thinking environment in order to create an opulent life. Your life is a reflection of your most dominant thoughts and meditations. When you make it a practice to meditate on success, you will begin to live a successful life.

The trouble for most people is that they don't know exactly what success would look like for them as individuals or, more importantly, what it would feel like personally. It is not enough just to meditate on success generally; you need to be specific. You are the architect and building contractor of your future. Use your thoughts as an architect uses a blueprint. Think about every detail. An architect not only thinks about the rooms in a house but also the types of windows, the size of closets, the location of outlets, and so on. Nothing is too insignificant. Think big and think detailed!

> **Your every present thought is a significant building block in determining the quality of your future.**

Ask Michael Dell. Borrowing one thousand dollars from family members at nineteen, he launched his multibillion-dollar company that dominates computer manufacturing today. On the premise that he could beat out large manufacturers by building custom computers and selling directly to consumers, he began selling systems and accessories out of his dorm room.[11] This radical idea shook the computer world to its foundations. How did he do it? He thought big, he thought detailed, and he thought outside of the box.

If you want your life to be different, you must dare to think differently—dare to think outside of the box. Think possibility thoughts. Remember, according to Mark 10:27, "with God all things are possible." Yes! Yes!

It could be for this very reason that Jabez, in 1 Chronicles 4:9–10, did not ask God for more property or greater wealth but to enlarge his intellectual territory—or his mental capacity regarding his own worth. He asked God to give him a greater capacity for conceiving what he might accomplish on God's behalf because he knew his own limited thinking was holding him captive. He prayed that God would give him a greater ability to think big. You need to cultivate possibility thinking because your thoughts determine your destiny. You have to be able to think about your future regarding what you really want to accomplish and on behalf of whom.

Determine now what steps you need to take on a daily basis to make the most of your life in the future. I like what Henry David Thoreau says: "Go confidently in the direction of your dreams. Live the life you have imagined."[12]

Nothing limits achievement like small thinking—nothing expands possibilities like thinking outside of the box. Unleash the power of your mind. Learn to cultivate possibility thinking. Think original thoughts. Think about something that has never been done, or put a new spin on something that has always been around. In 1886, John Pemberton turned common medicinal syrup into a cultural phenomenon by combining it with carbonated water and serving it as a refreshing drink. Coca-Cola is now the most widely known beverage on the planet.[13]

Bill Gates, the computer mogul, was determined to find a way to apply his skills in the computer industry. At Harvard, Gates would spend many long nights in front of the school's computer discussing ideas and the possibility of a future computer business with fellow student Paul Allen. When browsing through a magazine one day, Allen and Gates saw that the computer market was about to explode and that someone would have to make software for all those new machines. They acted on this hunch and worked on a program they thought had promise. Within the year, Bill Gates took a leave of absence from Harvard, and Microsoft was formed.[14] Sometimes you need to see with new eyes. The possibilities in your life change when your perspective changes. This is true vision.

Bill Gates was a visionary. He brought a fresh perspective to the world of computers. Vision connects you to your destiny and future. Helen Keller said, "The greatest tragedy in life is people who have sight but no vision."[15] You must see yourself doing more, gaining more, and being more. Vision is the ability to think progressively. A vision is a mental image of future possibilities. A friend of mine once told me that your feet will never take you where your mind has never been. Become the Christopher Columbus of your future. Columbus dared to lose sight of the known in order to experience the unknown. To conquer new territories you must have courage to lose sight of the shore. Dream big, then dare to wake up and accomplish it. Motivational speaker Robert J. Kriegel has said, "The shame in life is not to fail to reach your dream, but to fail to have a dream to reach."

## THINK BEYOND WHERE YOU ARE

If you want to progress in life, you have to think progressive thoughts. To do so, something new must replace the old. You have to think beyond where you are. Alexander Graham Bell thought beyond the limitation of the dots and dashes of the Morse code and replaced the telegraph with the innovation of the telephone. Become a visionary—be creative. Take the limits off your mind! Think beyond where you are.

"The shame in life is not to fail to reach your dream, but to fail to have a dream to reach."

As the narrator announced at the beginning of every episode of the cult-classic *Star Trek*, "Boldly go where no man has gone before." Dare to become the trailblazer of your own life.

God is a creative God; therefore, we are creative beings. We are made in His image. As His son or daughter you can tap into the creative mind of God—the genius of God—and see what other people cannot see and hear what other people cannot hear. Follow the example of Jesus:

> I tell you the truth, the Son can do nothing by himself; he can do only what he sees his Father doing, because whatever the Father does the Son also does. For the Father loves the Son and shows him all he does. Yes, to your amazement he will show him even greater things than these.
>
> —John 5:19–20, NIV

Jesus said that when other people were unable to see what was going on in heaven, He could. This is the challenge of creative thinking—as you open the spiritual channels of your mind, God can download divine, creative thoughts into your brain. Ask God to enlarge your capacity for thinking, to take the limits off.  Amen

God will not only grant you your prayerful requests, but He will also grant you your daily declarations. Just as Jabez altered his destiny by asking God to give him bigger thoughts, you can change yours, too. I challenge you to change your role from being a cheerleader to becoming a drum major. March to the beat of your own drum, to the rhythm of your individuality, and to the symphonic pulsating sounds of your unique destiny and purpose.

## DON'T UNDERESTIMATE
## THE POWER OF YOUR THOUGHTS

Whatever your predominant focus is, that is what you permit to exist in your life. Jabez chose to focus on his future desires rather than his present circumstances. Many times people focus on the negative, and they live in a cycle of negativity. You have to choose to focus on the positive. You have to train your mind to think on whatever is honest, virtuous, and praiseworthy. (See Philippians 4:8.) Whatever is going wrong in your life is a result of your focus. If you don't like it, change your focus!

In Genesis 13:14–18, God taught Abraham something about focus. He told him to look at the territory He was giving him, walk the land in every direction, and visualize the expanse of his legacy. Then He said to him, "I will make your descendants as the dust of the earth; so that if a man could number the dust of the earth, then your descendants also could be numbered" (v. 16). What did God train him to do? He trained him to focus on bigger thoughts.

If you plan to change your future, do not focus on things or people or circumstances that are smaller than what you are hoping for. Your focus will either feed your faith or confirm your fears. Learn to think like Abraham. Think intentionally, generationally, and even globally. You can never think too big, too grand, or too great! I challenge you with the words of Daniel H. Burnham:

> Make no little plans; they have no magic to stir men's blood and probably themselves will not be realized. Make big plans; aim high in hope and work, remembering that a noble, logical diagram once recorded will not die, but long after we are gone be a living thing, asserting itself with ever-growing insistence.[16]

Learn to think strategically as Solomon did in establishing his kingdom after David's reign. Purposefully seek God's wisdom so that He can download specific time-tables, goals, objectives, and resources into your mind. Listen to Solomon's prayer and how God responded as recorded in 2 Chronicles:

> Solomon said to God… "Give me now wisdom and knowledge to go out and come in before this people, for who can govern this people of yours, which is so great?"
>
> God answered Solomon, "Because this was in your heart, and you have not asked possessions, wealth, honor, or the life of those who hate you, and have not even asked long life, but have asked wisdom and knowledge for yourself that you may govern my people over whom I have made you king, wisdom and knowledge are granted to you.

I will also give you riches, possessions, and honor, such as none of the kings had who were before you, and none after you shall have the like."

—2 Chronicles 1:8, 10–12, ESV

## CREATE A CREATIVE ENVIRONMENT

One thing I do that helps me to think more strategically and wisely, and therefore to pray more effectively, is to be mindful about my environment. Your environment will impact your attitude, focus, faith, and the intentionality of your thoughts. If you are surrounded by clutter, noise, reminders of lack, and other problems, you will find it more difficult to think past those limiting issues. You have the power to create an inspirational environment around yourself.

I like beauty—anything that's beautiful, clean, and orderly automatically gives me inspiration. Some people like the quiet of nature or the stimulation of music or a bustling café. God gave man a myriad of inspirational environments to spur his creativity. Look for those particular environments that inspire thoughts of abundance on every level, and find a way to spend blocks of time in your most creative space.

**Your success and prosperity hinge on what lies within your mind.**

When you find that place, practice thinking "divergently," outside of the box, and see yourself taking some risks. The biggest risk in life is not taking any risk at all! Prepare your mind to seek after and accept greater challenges. If you have trouble thinking outside of the box, then imagine creating a new one. Practice thinking like an entrepreneur, and become comfortable with thoughts of achievement and success—think and feel as if you already have what you desire. Create the feelings of success by pretending you are living the kind of life you have imagined until this practice affects the habits of your mind. Think in the present; think positively—see the thing that you want, the business you hope to accomplish, the person you plan to marry, and so on, as if you are already in possession of what you desire. Condition your mind to accept these thoughts, and you will draw these opportunities and experiences to yourself.

Your success and prosperity hinge on what lies within your mind. The first thing that you need to change is your thoughts about what God wants for you. He wants you to live a life of abundance. It is His desire to give you divine universal secrets to great success and prosperity. He holds the secret spiritual recipe for abundant living.

There are many people who may not be as spiritual as you are, but nevertheless they were able to tap into something great. Whether by accident or providence, they are living lives beyond their wildest dreams, and you can, too. You must say to yourself, until this one fact becomes your conviction, "God wants me to live in abundance!"

A world of possibilities is waiting to be released in your future. Amen

> Jesus said to him, "If you can believe, all things are possible to him who believes."
>
> —Mark 9:23

# CHAPTER THREE

# THE CREATIVE POWER OF SPOKEN WORDS

For those men who, sooner or later, are lucky enough to break away from the pack, the most intoxicating moment comes when they cease being bodies in other men's command and find that they control their own time, when they learn their own voice and authority.[1]

—Theodore White

CONSCIOUSLY CHOOSING YOUR WORDS IS LIKE putting together the right combination of bricks and mortar. Just as the great architects have taken raw materials to build skyscrapers and timeless monuments, your words are the raw materials that can form the life you are meant to live. Words carry great power, and Scripture is replete with principles that support the power of the tongue. Job 22:28 states:

You will also declare a thing,
And it will be established for you;
So light will shine on your ways.

This scripture refers to your royal anointing—the favor God has poured over you because you belong to Him. It reminds me of the story when Samuel went to David and poured anointing oil over his head to signify he would be the next king of Israel. Samuel didn't bring him a crown, but he anointed him with oil—a symbol of the Holy Spirit and God's blessings and approval. It was many years later before David actually wore that crown, but from the moment he was anointed, he was already a king in God's eyes. Good things began to happen to him almost immediately because he started looking at his world through eyes of blessing rather than eyes of failure. Even as he overcame the lion and the bear, he knew he could overcome giants. And just as he took authority and overcame everything that threatened his ascent to the throne, you must take authority and overcome everything that threatens your ascent into the realm of success and prosperity.

A king does not beg and cry for anything. He does not have to. He declares something, and that thing is established. A king has the legal power to *decree*, which is an old English word for "legislate." He institutes, he confirms, he settles, he summons, he authorizes—that's what a king does.

Peter tells us we belong to "a royal priesthood" (1 Pet. 2:9). The word *royal* speaks of our kingly attributes as believers. Remember, Jesus is King of kings—He is the capital-"K" King, and we are the lowercase-"k" kings. You must manifest your royal anointing to decree blessings over your marriage, family, business, ministry, and every other realm of your life.

The whole universe is waiting for us to give it instruction. As the Bible says, "For the earnest expectation of the creation eagerly waits for the revealing of the sons of God" (Rom. 8:19). The whole universe waits in anticipation for the sons and daughters of God to manifest themselves and bring it back into alignment with God's original intent for them. Every word you speak is pregnant with regal, creative power.

> You must manifest your royal anointing to decree blessings over your marriage, family, business, ministry, and every other realm of your life.

The first to illustrate this was God Himself. According to Hebrews 11:3, "The universe was created by the word of God, so that *what is seen was not made out of things that are visible*" (ESV, emphasis added). Words are the "things" that this verse is referring to. Even though words are not visible, they are substantive entities that brought tangibility to the universe through the power of God.

In the first chapter of the Book of Genesis, we see at the beginning of each day of the creation story, "And God said, 'Let there be…'" God spoke out what He had seen in His mind as He had dreamed about creating the universe, and when He spoke, the earth, all the planets, the sun, moon, and stars, as well as every plant, animal, and humanity itself, appeared just as He had seen us all in His mind's eye. God spoke, and from seemingly "nothingness" came everything that exists in the physical universe.

## A DEEPER UNDERSTANDING

James, the brother of Jesus, explained how this is to work in our lives:

> For we all stumble in many ways, and if anyone does not stumble in what he says, he is a perfect man, able also to bridle his whole body. If we put bits into the mouths of horses so that they obey us, we guide their whole bodies as well. Look at the ships also: though they are so large and are driven by strong winds, they are guided by a very small rudder wherever the will of the pilot directs. So also the tongue is a small member, yet it boasts of great things.
> —James 3:2–5, ESV

When a ship sets sail to cross the sea, the pilot plots out the course. Then he determines the times he will need to adjust the direction of the ship to follow the course he has set. He checks his calculations from time to time to ensure he is always headed in the right direction, and then he keeps the steering as steady as possible, heading toward his predetermined destination. Certainly along the way he may have to adjust the helm to go around storms, navigate currents, or avoid obstacles in the water, but he always steers with his focus more on where he is going than what he is going through. If he constantly changes the steering from one minute to the next, fixating on his present circumstances, the ship is more likely to go in circles than it is to arrive at the desired port of call.

For the pilot, the course is created first in his thoughts, communicated through the rudder, and then realized as the rest of the ship lines up with his intent. For us, our lives only arrive at our desired goals if we line up our thoughts, words, habits, and actions in a similar way. With this framework in mind, you can choose to live consciously and intentionally. Rather than letting the elements of your day dictate your destiny, you can take control of these elements and direct their course to a greater end.

You must take the time to consider carefully the course of your life. Where are you heading? What will it look like when you get there? Let your imagination take over. Spend time daydreaming about where you want to be in life. Read about it. Study that place. Write about it in your journal. Draw it. Paint it. Let your mind run free with the possibilities of what you can attain, what you can be, and what you can accomplish. Transform your imaginations into intentions. Act intentionally rather than react unconsciously.

What will it take to get there? Are there skills you will need to acquire? Are there people who live in that place whom you can learn from? How did they get there? What paths did they take? Are there habits you should form that will keep you on course?

Now talk about it. Line up your mouth—the rudder of your life—with where you are going. Then keep it steady and on course.

What happens to a ship if you head it in one direction at one moment, and then turn it in the opposite direction in the next—and keep doing that over and over? Pretty simple—it goes nowhere. This is what happens when people start speaking about the good things they are expecting to happen one minute and then spend the next half hour talking about all the negative things happening to them that are keeping them from getting there. They are turning their lives in circles. They line up their spoken words with where they want to go for a little while; then when they meet a storm along the way, all they do is talk about the bad weather and lose track of where they were headed in the first place. They forget that they have the power to turn their lives around in the storm or press on through it to the sunshine on the other side.

> **Even in the midst of what looks like catastrophe, keep speaking the blessing; keep the ship of your life on a steady course, and before you know it, the storm clouds will clear and you will have broken through your difficulty and left it far behind you.**

They forget that the "Son" has never stopped shining on their lives, no matter how dark the clouds in the sky are.

Even in the midst of what looks like catastrophe, keep speaking the blessing; keep the ship of your life on a steady course, and before you know it, the storm clouds will clear and you will have broken through your difficulty and left it far behind you.

## TELL YOUR TROUBLES WHERE TO GO

Your every decree is pregnant with the power and potential to revolutionize your life. Psalm 2:7–8 indicates that God utilizes this prerogative and grants the same to His earthly ambassadors:

> I will declare the decree:
> The LORD has said to Me,
> "You are My Son,
> Today I have begotten You.
> Ask of Me, and I will give You
> The nations for your inheritance
> And the ends of the earth for Your possession."

David used his right to decree and declare to turn the tides of Israel's unfavorable fate and to defeat their enemy Goliath. In 1 Samuel 17:46–51, David addresses his enemy with conviction and authority:

"This day the LORD will deliver you into my hand, and I will strike you and take your head from you. And this day I will give the carcasses of the camp of the Philistines to the birds of the air and the wild beasts of the earth, that all the earth may know that there is a God in Israel. Then all this assembly shall know that the LORD does not save with sword and spear; for the battle is the LORD's, and He will give you into our hands."

So it was, when the Philistine arose and came and drew near to meet David, that David hurried and ran toward the army to meet the Philistine. Then David put his hand in his bag and took out a stone; and he slung it and struck the Philistine in his forehead, so that the stone sank into his forehead, and he fell on his face to the earth. So David prevailed over the Philistine with a sling and a stone, and struck the Philistine and killed him....David ran and stood over the Philistine, took his sword...out of its sheath...and cut off his head with it. And when the Philistines saw that their champion was dead, they fled.

Since the spirit realm is the causal realm, Goliath was dead long before he was struck by the stone and beheaded by the sword.

Remember, according to Proverbs 18:21, "Death and life are in the power of the tongue, and those who love it will eat its fruit." Choose to use your tongue to bring life and not death, to bless and not to curse—even when it comes to your "enemies." Learn the art of blessing, for in blessing a thing or a person, that thing or person must bless you: "Bless those who persecute you; bless and do not curse" (Rom. 12:14). When you bless, blessings will be drawn to you, or as Deuteronomy 28:2 says, "Blessings shall come upon you and overtake you." Conversely, in cursing a thing or a person, you draw curses upon yourself. *Ouch*

Again, as James said, "A double-minded man [is] unstable in all his ways" (James 1:8). What did he mean? A double-minded person is a person with conflicting thoughts—someone who holds two different opinions at the same time. That person is the pilot who steers his ship toward one port for a while, then reverses to steer it toward another in the opposite direction. "He…is like a wave of the sea driven and tossed by the wind" (v. 6). At one point your life is headed toward blessings because that is what you have spoken, and the next it is headed toward cursing because that is now what your mouth is proclaiming.

James again describes this pilot's plight later in his letter:

> With it [the tongue] we bless our God and Father, and with it we curse men, who have been made in the similitude of God. Out of the same mouth proceed blessing and cursing. My brethren, these things ought not to be so.
>
> —James 3:9–10

I am convinced that, because of ignorance, believers tend to live beneath the standard God has ordained for His children. We do not know that our daily declarations and decrees have the power to alter our destiny and change the quality of our lives. Proverbs 13:3 states that, "He who guards his mouth [watches what he says] preserves his life." Or again as James said, "If anyone does not stumble in word, he is a perfect [mature] man, able also to bridle the whole body" (James 3:2). If guarding your words causes you to keep your life and grow in maturity, imagine what happens when you do not guard your words.

Here is an example of someone whose mouth prevented him from tasting the blessing.

> Then Elisha said, "Hear the word of the LORD. Thus says the LORD: 'Tomorrow about this time a seah of fine flour shall be sold for a shekel, and two seahs of barley for a shekel, at the gate of Samaria.'" So an officer on whose hand the king leaned answered the man of God and said, "Look, if the LORD would make windows in heaven [spiritual portals], could this thing be?" And he said, "In fact, you shall see it with your eyes, but you shall not eat of it."
>
> Now there were four leprous men at the entrance of the gate; and they said to one another, "Why are we sitting here until we die? If we say, 'We will enter the city,' the famine is in the city, and we shall die there. And if we sit here, we die also.

Now therefore, come, let us surrender to the army of the Syrians. If they keep us alive, we shall live; and if they kill us, we shall but die." And they rose at twilight to go to the camp of the Syrians; and when they had come to the outskirts of the Syrian camp, to their surprise no one was there.... They went into one tent and ate and drank, and carried from it silver and gold and clothing, and went and hid them; then they came back and entered another tent, and carried some from there also, and went and hid it.

Then they said to one another, "We are not doing what is right. This day is a day of good news, and we remain silent. If we wait until morning light, some punishment will come upon us. Now therefore, come, let us go and tell the king's household." So they went and called to the gatekeepers of the city, and told them, saying, "We went to the Syrian camp, and surprisingly no one was there, not a human sound—only horses and donkeys tied, and the tents intact." And the gatekeepers called out, and they told it to the king's household inside....

Now the king had appointed the officer on whose hand he leaned to have charge of the gate. But the people trampled him in the gate, and he died, just as the man of God had said, who spoke when the king came down to him. So it happened just as the man of God had spoken to the king, saying, "Two seahs of barley for a shekel, and a seah of fine flour for a shekel, shall be sold tomorrow about this time in the gate of Samaria."

—2 Kings 7:1–5, 8–11, 17–18

The prophet Elisha spoke the blessing of God into manifestation. It took one prophetic declaration to change the economic landscape of an entire nation. The officer who influenced the king met divine declaration with skepticism and unbelief. His words literally aborted the blessing of God for him and caused him instead to lose his life. This man died because he refused to agree with the plan of God and scoffed at the methodology of a blessing. However, four lepers, who weren't even in close proximity to the declaration, prospered by it. They experienced a supernatural supply because of a prophetic explosion that opened the windows of heaven.

## SPEAK OUT YOUR BLESSINGS

Hosea 8:7 states, "They sow the wind and reap the whirlwind" (NIV). This demonstrates the powerful nature of words. Whatever you sow will come back to you multiplied.

Place your hand directly in front of your mouth and declare aloud, "I am blessed, all of my needs are met, and I have more than enough for myself, my household, and extra left over to give to others."

Did you feel the power of those words coming forth

out of your mouth like a breeze? Those same words will come back to you, manifested with hurricane force, blowing into your life abundance and blessings or lack and calamity depending on what you spoke out.

Choose to steer your life into blessings by filling the atmosphere around you with words of faith and victory.

> Do not be deceived, God is not mocked; for whatever a man sows, that he will also reap. For he who sows to his flesh will of the flesh reap corruption, but he who sows to the Spirit will of the Spirit reap everlasting life.
>
> —Galatians 6:7–8

# CHAPTER FOUR

# WHAT HAVE YOU PUT IN THE ATMOSPHERE?

I am the sum total of what I have been confessing through the years.[1]

—Joel Osteen

ORDS RELEASED INTO THE ATMOSPHERE DO not disappear and dissipate. They have no geographical limitations. Words have power, presence, and prophetic implications. They create a magnetic force that pulls the manifestation of what you speak—good or bad, blessing or cursing—from other realms, regions, and dimensions. They are suspended and incubated in the realm of the spirit awaiting the correct time and optimum condition for manifestation.

Joshua released just such a declaration after the conquest of Jericho. He said:

> Cursed be the man before the LORD who rises up and builds this city Jericho; he shall lay its foundation with his firstborn, and with his youngest he shall set up its gates.
>
> —Joshua 6:26

These words hung in the atmosphere for approximately six hundred years without anything happening in Jericho. Then 1 Kings 16:34 tells the rest of the story:

> In his days Hiel of Bethel built Jericho. He laid its foundation with Abiram his firstborn, and with his youngest son Segub he set up its gates, according to the word of the LORD, which He had spoken through Joshua the son of Nun.

Did you get that? The death of Hiel's firstborn and youngest occurred as a result of words released out of the mouth of Joshua and of the corresponding action of Hiel.

Again, in the Book of Numbers (a story we have already touched on briefly) the children of Israel wandered in the wilderness for forty years and died, not because they were lost, but because they legislated their wandering exile with their own mouths. Because of their capricious, negative, and ungrateful chatter, they ignorantly altered their destiny from a journey that should have lasted approximately a fortnight to one of forty years. Was this fate of the devil, the original plan of God, or their own doing? Scripture clearly reveals that the forty-year wilderness journey occurred as a result of their own ensnaring words:

> All the children of Israel complained against Moses and Aaron, and the whole congregation said to them, "If only we had died in the land of

Egypt! Or if only we had died in this wilderness! Why has the LORD brought us to this land to fall by the sword, that our wives and children should become victims? Would it not be better for us to return to Egypt?"...

But Joshua the son of Nun and Caleb the son of Jephunneh, who were among those who had spied out the land, tore their clothes; and they spoke to all the congregation of the children of Israel, saying: "The land we passed through to spy out is an exceedingly good land. If the LORD delights in us, then He will bring us into this land and give it to us, 'a land which flows with milk and honey.' Only do not rebel against the LORD, nor fear the people of the land, for they are our bread; their protection has departed from them, and the LORD is with us. Do not fear them." And all the congregation said to stone them with stones. Now the glory of the LORD appeared in the tabernacle of meeting before all the children of Israel.

Then the LORD said to Moses: "How long will these people reject Me? And how long will they not believe Me, with all the signs which I have performed among them?"

—Numbers 14:2–3, 6–11

God had spoken good things over the people of Israel and promised to give them the land of Canaan for their inheritance. However, they trusted more in their own fears than in God. They trusted more in the comfort of slavery than in the hope of living as kings and priests. Though God had promised them their own land, they undid His promises not only with their lack of faith but also with the words they spoke.

In fact, while they were camping on the banks of the Jordan, looking into Canaan with their knees knocking together in cowardice, those in Canaan were looking at them with trepidations of their own. Forty years later, when Joshua and Caleb returned with the new generation of Israelites to collect on God's promise to them, they heard what the Canaanites had been saying of them when they had first spied out that land. As Rahab of Jericho told the spies:

**Words have power, presence, and prophetic implications.**

> I know that the LORD has given you the land, that the terror of you has fallen on us, and that all the inhabitants of the land are fainthearted because of you. For we have heard how the LORD dried up the water of the Red Sea for you when you came out of Egypt, and what you did to the two kings of the Amorites who were on the other side of the Jordan, Sihon and Og, whom you utterly destroyed. And as soon as we heard these things, our hearts melted; neither did there remain any more courage in

anyone because of you, for the LORD your God, He
is God in heaven above and on earth beneath.

—Joshua 2:9–11

While the Israelites were calling those in Canaan
"giants," the hearts of those "giants" were melting in
fear of the Israelites! Instead of listening to Joshua and
Caleb, whose words filled the atmosphere with faith,
they chose instead to suck all hope from their surroundings by listening instead to the other ten spies who spoke
only of their inability and the greatness of their enemies.
They even tried to repent when they realized what they
had done and decided to try to obey God in taking the
land, but it was too late—their own words had already
undone them.

> "As I live," says the LORD, "just as you have spoken
> in My hearing, so I will do to you: The carcasses
> of you who have complained against Me shall fall
> in this wilderness, all of you who were numbered,
> according to your entire number, from twenty
> years old and above. Except for Caleb the son of
> Jephunneh and Joshua the son of Nun, you shall
> by no means enter the land which I swore I would
> make you dwell in. But your little ones, whom you
> said would be victims, I will bring in, and they
> shall know the land which you have despised...."
>
> Then Moses told these words to all the children
> of Israel, and the people mourned greatly. And

they rose early in the morning and went up to the top of the mountain, saying, "Here we are, and we will go up to the place which the LORD has promised, for we have sinned!" And Moses said, "Now why do you transgress the command of the LORD? For this will not succeed. Do not go up, lest you be defeated by your enemies, for the LORD is not among you. For the Amalekites and the Canaanites are there before you, and you shall fall by the sword; because you have turned away from the LORD, the LORD will not be with you." But they presumed to go up to the mountaintop. Nevertheless, neither the ark of the covenant of the LORD nor Moses departed from the camp. Then the Amalekites and the Canaanites who dwelt in that mountain came down and attacked them, and drove them back as far as Hormah.

—Numbers 14:28–31, 39–45

Even though they were acting on God's word to them, they filled the atmosphere with their own fear and defeat rather than faith and victory. What they received was not according to God's promises but according to what they filled the atmosphere with. They steered their lives into a port of fear and failure, dropped anchor there—and then they were surprised that the water was filled with nothing but sharks. They snatched defeat right out of the mouth of victory.

Just like these Israelites, are you getting exactly what you have always been asking for?

## WORDS WORTH AGREEING WITH

When you read one of God's promises to you in the Bible, what is your first thought? Do you think, "Oh, it will be wonderful to have that someday in heaven," or "What a wonderful promise! Of course, that is not for someone as miserable as me." Or do you think, "Praise God! If He says that I should have that, then nothing can stop His blessing from manifesting in my life!"

Unfortunately, too many pick the first two. Just like the Israelites standing on the bank of the Jordan looking at what was promised them, we too often choose to give up before the battle even begins.

Did you know that some of the greatest Christians of all times were lawyers? Now, we tend to make fun of lawyers and politicians in our culture today, but throughout history, lawyers have revealed some of the greatest things about God we have ever known. Moses was "the lawgiver," and the apostle Paul was a Pharisee. (The Pharisees were a group who

> Come into agreement with what God has already said in His Word about you and your situation. You have to get God's Word on it. Then fill your atmosphere with His promises on the matter.

studied the Word of God as the law book on which to govern society.) Martin Luther of the Reformation began his career by entering law school, as did the great revivalist Charles Finney. What made them so powerful? They read their Bibles as lawyers would when studying to prepare a case, and they put more faith in God keeping His Word than they did in any earthly laws or political promises. Then they took those words and charged the atmosphere around them with biblical truth. They changed their worlds through what they spoke.

Look what happened when Ezekiel took God at His Word and spoke it into a dead atmosphere:

> The hand of the LORD came upon me and brought me out in the Spirit of the LORD, and set me down in the midst of the valley; and it was full of bones. Then He caused me to pass by them all around, and behold, there were very many in the open valley; and indeed they were very dry. And He said to me, "Son of man, can these bones live?" So I answered, "O Lord GOD, You know." Again He said to me, "Prophesy to these bones, and say to them, 'O dry bones, hear the word of the LORD! Thus says the Lord GOD to these bones: "Surely I will cause breath to enter into you, and you shall live. I will put sinews on you and bring flesh upon you, cover you with skin and put breath in you; and you shall live. Then you shall know that I am the LORD."'"

So I prophesied as I was commanded; and as I prophesied, there was a noise, and suddenly a rattling; and the bones came together, bone to bone. Indeed, as I looked, the sinews and the flesh came upon them, and the skin covered them over; but there was no breath in them. Then He said to me, "Prophesy to the breath, prophesy, son of man, and say to the breath, 'Thus says the Lord God: "Come from the four winds, O breath, and breathe on these slain, that they may live."'" So I prophesied as He commanded me, and breath came into them, and they lived, and stood upon their feet, an exceedingly great army.

Then He said to me, "Son of man, these bones are the whole house of Israel. They indeed say, 'Our bones are dry, our hope is lost, and we ourselves are cut off!' Therefore prophesy and say to them, 'Thus says the Lord God: "Behold, O My people, I will open your graves and cause you to come up from your graves, and bring you into the land of Israel. Then you shall know that I am the Lord, when I have opened your graves, O My people, and brought you up from your graves. I will put My Spirit in you, and you shall live, and I will place you in your own land. Then you shall know that I, the Lord, have spoken it and performed it," says the Lord.'"

—Ezekiel 37:1–14

When you read the Bible, you need to take God's Word personally. His promises are for His people, and if you have given your life to Him as your Lord and Savior, then that means YOU. Speak life into your dead areas—you'll be amazed at what God's words in your mouth will do for you.

If God has said it, then that should settle it for us.

## THE BATTLE BELONGS TO THE LORD

Second Chronicles, chapter 20, tells the story of King Jehoshaphat as Israel faced invasion from a coalition of nations lead by the Moabites and the Ammonites:

> Some came and told Jehoshaphat, saying, "A great multitude is coming against you from beyond the sea, from Syria; and they are in Hazazon Tamar" (which is En Gedi). And Jehoshaphat feared, and set himself to seek the LORD, and proclaimed a fast throughout all Judah....
>
> Then Jehoshaphat stood in the assembly of Judah and Jerusalem, in the house of the LORD, before the new court, and said: "O LORD God of our fathers, are You not God in heaven, and do You not rule over all the kingdoms of the nations, and in Your hand is there not power and might, so that no one is able to withstand You?...O our God, will You not judge them? For we have no power against this great multitude that is coming

against us; nor do we know what to do, but our eyes are upon You."...

Then the Spirit of the LORD came upon Jahaziel....And he said, "Listen, all you of Judah and you inhabitants of Jerusalem, and you, King Jehoshaphat! Thus says the LORD to you: 'Do not be afraid nor dismayed because of this great multitude, for the battle is not yours, but God's....You will not need to fight in this battle. Position yourselves, stand still and see the salvation of the LORD, who is with you, O Judah and Jerusalem!' Do not fear or be dismayed; tomorrow go out against them, for the LORD is with you."...

So they rose early in the morning and went out into the Wilderness of Tekoa; and as they went out, Jehoshaphat stood and said, "Hear me, O Judah and you inhabitants of Jerusalem: Believe in the LORD your God [come into agreement with what God is saying], and you shall be established [to be upheld, nourished, settled and able to stand firm]; believe [come into agreement with what the prophets are saying—because with God, nothing is impossible] His prophets, and you shall prosper [prevail, succeed, advance, progress, and overcome]." And when he had consulted with the people, he appointed those who should sing to the LORD, and who should praise the beauty of holiness, as they went out before the army and were saying: "Praise the LORD, for His mercy endures forever."

Now when they began to sing and to praise, the LORD set ambushes against the people of Ammon, Moab, and Mount Seir, who had come against Judah; and they were defeated.

—2 Chronicles 20:2–3, 5–6, 12, 14–15, 20–22

Rather than fear, Jehoshaphat got God's plan and put it into action. He took God at His word that the battle was His. Then they celebrated God's salvation before they even saw it. They filled their atmosphere with praise and worship, charging the air with God's power and provision, and by the time they saw their enemies, they were already defeated.

Come into agreement with what God has already said in His Word about you and your situation. You have to get God's Word on it. Then fill your atmosphere with His promises on the matter.

Let us hold fast the confession of our hope without wavering, for He who promised is faithful. Amen

—Hebrews 10:23

CHAPTER FIVE

# YOU CAN CHANGE THE COURSE OF YOUR DESTINY

A man sooner or later discovers that he is the master-gardener of his soul, the director of his life.[1]
—James Allen

AS WE LEARNED FROM HEBREWS 11:3, ANYTHING you are able to see was made from that which is not seen. This is an amazing concept, and it is what makes the biblical truths about spiritual reality so fascinating. There is nothing that currently exists that has not always been. That means whatever you are able to experience with your five senses was "brought forth" from the spiritual realm; it was made manifest by the power of God, and it's that same power that works in and through you. I say "made manifest" because that is how creation works. Knowing there is a cause for every effect, we know something "is" because it has been "brought forth." Without a thing being conceived in the mind and spoken out—without calling those things that are not as though they were (Rom. 4:17)—nothing that exists would exist.

This might sound mystical and New Age, but the

principle of thought and word framing reality is found from the first book of the Bible to the last. It is in the story of Creation. It is in the new heaven and the new earth that are to come.

God created the tangible, temporal world by calling it forth. He gave form to what physicists have come to call "substance"—the "essential nature," as *Webster's Dictionary* says, that makes up the unseen world—by changing the composition of raw energy with the power of His decrees and declarations. God didn't bring the world into being from nothingness; rather He brought everything into existence from matter that already existed within Himself.

> By changing His intention, focusing His thoughts, and harnessing His words, God set the universe in motion. Though it is to a lesser extent, we create our personal universe in the same way.

> For by Him all things were created that are in heaven and that are on earth, visible and invisible....All things were created through Him and for Him. And He is before all things, and *in Him all things consist.*
> —Colossians 1:16–17, emphasis added

The Latin root of *creation* is literally "to bring forth." Through the power of His thoughts and words, God "brought forth" what was in Him out into the physical world.

So rather than thinking about the process of creation as making something out of nothing, for our benefit we should think of it as tapping into an unlimited source of energy in the spiritual realm to bring forth what we have imagined possible. God set the universe in motion by changing His intention, focusing His thoughts, and harnessing His words. Though it is to a lesser extent, we create our personal universe in the same way.

## THE SCIENCE OF FAITH

Invisible to our naked eye are the molecules hydrogen and oxygen, yet through a chemical reaction they become a visible substance called water. The same happens with sodium and chloride coming together to form table salt. In this physical, or chemical, realm, God set these invisible processes in motion at Creation to respond continuously to His word to form visible substances that add to our life. He has done the same in the spiritual realm. Every moment of every day we are surrounded by spiritual "molecules" that are designed to respond to our thoughts and intentions—or more scripturally put, our faith—to produce miracles. As Scripture puts it, "And this is the victory that has overcome the world—our faith" (1 John 5:4). Everything you need for victory already exists, but it exists in another form. Since the spirit realm is the causal realm, then your miracle is always in motion—you just need to get it to manifest on your behalf! However, just as you can bring it forth with your faith-filled thoughts and words, you can also stall it out by speaking out your doubt and dwelling on unbelief.

Let's look at the example Jesus gave us when He performed His miracle of multiplication in Matthew 14:19–20:

> He took the five loaves and the two fish, and looking up to heaven, He blessed and broke and gave the loaves to the disciples; and the disciples gave to the multitudes. So they all ate and were filled, and they took up twelve baskets full of the fragments that remained.

Jesus multiplied the bread and the fish by speaking to it and blessing it. He turned His eyes toward heaven and spoke out a blessing. The verb for *bless* here means "to invoke God's presence" as well as "to infuse His provision into a thing." He invoked God's presence, and the bread and fish were "brought forth" or "made manifest"—Jesus affected the spiritual "molecules" enough to cause the bread and fish to miraculously appear—but they had been there the whole time in the spiritual realm.

## GOD'S PROMISES COME THROUGH FAITH AND PERSISTENCE

In Daniel 10:12 we read about the angel who came as a result of Daniel's words:

> Do not fear, Daniel, for from the first day that you set your heart to understand, and to humble yourself before your God, your words were heard; and I have come because of your words.

When Daniel prayed, God sent the answer immediately, but there were forces that prohibited it from being manifested right away. We read in the next verse the angel's explanation for the delay: "The prince of the kingdom of Persia withstood me twenty-one days" (v. 13). As Daniel had persisted in prayer, the angel had persisted in his warring. Even though Daniel did not see any sign of the answer manifesting during all that time, it was in motion. Eventually it did come into being because Daniel never stopped praying and decreeing. The answer broke through because Daniel stood firm in his faith and his confession. Remember, there are always forces at work prohibiting your answer from manifesting. If you don't sabotage your prayers with negative thoughts and words, then you will eventually see with your eyes the substance of what you have hoped for just as Daniel did.

You need to understand that there are laws of incubation

and manifestation that govern your miracle. Just because a baby is hidden within its mother for nine months does not mean it isn't there—the embryo once it is conceived must undergo a season of incubation before manifestation occurs. In the same way a seed is buried in the ground and can go weeks without an apparent change before it sprouts, and then months more before it bears fruit.

So many times we declare a thing and then lose patience because it doesn't manifest like popcorn in a microwave! We need to realize that, when it doesn't come to pass immediately, we can undo what we have set in motion if we choose to speak words of discouragement instead of words filled with faith. Just because we don't see a thing come to pass in a certain period of time does not mean that it isn't ever going to be or that it isn't God's will. Remember how Joshua spoke a word and it took six hundred years before that particular word was manifested? Sometimes it takes a duration of time. We need to believe and speak as if it is coming today but stay strong and persist in our faith even if it takes decades.

Words don't just disappear once they are released into the atmosphere. They remain dormant there, incubating until the time for them to bear fruit is at hand. It could be they will be activated by someone else who will trigger a catalyst in the realm of the spirit in order for what you are hoping for to be made manifest. It could be there are opposing forces that require your perseverance, as was the case with Daniel. It could be any number of things delaying what God wants for you, but God kept it simple—regardless of the *why*, you need to keep your thoughts, your words, and your faith in line with what you are expecting, and then trust God to take care of the rest.

Too many people release careless words into the atmosphere and can't figure out why the life God has promised them isn't happening the way they hoped it would. Scripture has revealed to us that everything in the universe has to adjust itself to accommodate our words—good or bad, purposeful or errant. (See Proverbs 13:3; 18:21; 21:23.) This is why we read in Matthew 12:36 that every idle word—words with no kingdom assignment—will be brought into judgment. You will be held accountable for every idle word, but you will also be rewarded for every faith-filled word.

## THE POWER OF PROACTIVE PERMISSION

When God made the declaration, "Let there be light," He was really saying, "I allow light to be." He was giving the light, straining at its harnesses to exist in the spirit, permission to manifest itself in the physical world. We must understand there are prohibiting, spiritual forces at work able to keep these things from occurring. There are fallen angels that cause deviations to what God originally purposed working in opposition to what God wants for your life—they operate much like the heavenly angels assigned to bring about the manifestation to your prayers, only in the exact opposite way. According to Scripture, demonic forces were once angels who had been given the same original assignment of responding to voice-activated commands, but when they fell from heaven, their mission became perverted. So instead of bringing the answers, they prohibit answers from manifesting. Your faith attracts the attention of heaven's angels to work on your behalf, while your fear draws the demons of hell to work against you. Your words become the magnet that draws either heaven or hell into your situation.

Always remember, no force is more powerful than the spoken word of God. The Bible says the power of life and death is in your tongue (Prov. 18:21). It is the word of God that comes forth from your mouth that pulls all the resources of heaven into your situation. (See Matthew 18:18.) In her book *Live a Praying Life*, Jennifer Kennedy Dean writes, "In response to our prayers, spiritual forces are set in motion that bring God's will to earth. Prayer has its first effect in the spiritual realm. When the work is finished in the spiritual realm, the answer is revealed in the material realm."[2]

John Wesley once said, "It seems God is limited by our prayer life—that He can do nothing for humanity unless someone ask Him."[3] Throughout the Bible we learn that God cannot intervene on the earth unless someone gives permission for the answer to exist in the material world. Answers are held up in the heavenlies and locked up in the realm of the spirit until there is a person able to pick up on the correct frequency and act as a conduit to release God's will into the earth.

This is illustrated by Jacob's experience in the Book of Genesis. God gave Jacob a vision where he saw a ladder going up to heaven—the top of the ladder touched heaven and the bottom touched the earth. There were angels ascending and descending—much like radio waves moving along an antenna. This is exactly how divine inspiration works. Here God was speaking to Jacob's mind and enabling him to pick up a spiritual frequency. When he got tuned in to this frequency, he saw how the invisible realm was manifesting itself in the visible realm.

Sometimes our thoughts are like these frequencies. Jacob saw a ladder, and that was the modern technology of his day. But in the twenty-first century he might have seen a wireless computer or cell phone. Jacob was able to get a glimpse of a spiritual superhighway. I believe these superhighways are our thoughts—this is where we pick up inspiration—these inspirational thoughts seem to appear out of thin air, but really they are circulating in the realm of the spirit.

God gave Moses a vision of the heavenly tabernacle.

He gave Moses a vision of something that already existed in heaven—the actual spiritual tabernacle. God opened up the eyes of Moses, and he was able to see it and replicate it here on the earth. Secret things belong unto God, but those things that are revealed belong unto man. (See Deuteronomy 29:29.) It is a point of revelation—a point of inspiration—where God wants to speak to us all. He said, "I know the thoughts that I think toward you...thoughts of peace, and not of evil, to give you an expected end" (Jer. 29:11, KJV). He knows the end from the beginning, and He knows everything in between—and those are the things that He wants to reveal to you. Amen.

## TAKING HOLD OF THE WHEEL

In Job 38, God is asking Job a series of questions. At one point God asks, "Where were you...when the morning stars sang together?" (vv. 4, 7). Further down He inquires, "Have you commanded the morning since your days began?" (v. 12). In a sense, God is asking Job, "Have you thought about speaking into your morning and bringing order into your day?"

The Bible says:

> Eye has not seen, nor ear heard, nor have entered into the heart of man the things which God has prepared for those who love Him.
>
> —1 Corinthians 2:9

If these things are prepared but we have not received them, it could mean we have not done our part in bringing them forth. Think of Abraham stepping out in faith in obedience to God.

God said He wanted Abraham to sacrifice his most precious treasure—his son Isaac. As they moved toward the place of sacrifice, as Abraham lifted his hand to carry out God's instructions, there appeared a ram caught in the thicket. God provided the alternative, but not until Abraham moved out in obedience. The provision would not have appeared had Abraham not taken the first step. Many times God is expecting the corresponding action from us in order to bring these things to pass. What are you doing to prepare for the thing you have been declaring and believing for? How do your actions correspond to your belief that a certain event will come to pass as a result of the integrity of God's Word?

"Have you commanded the morning since your days began?" (Job 38:12). In a sense, God is asking Job, "Have you thought about speaking into your morning and bringing order into your day?"

In Deuteronomy 28:1–14, God declares a long list of blessings that will result if you heed His voice. Just as God declares a thing, He expects you, as king and priest, to do the same. Another way to say it is that His blessings are voice activated. Listen to what is written in Job 22:27–28:

> You will make your prayer to Him,
> He will hear you,
> And you will pay your vows.
> You will also declare a thing,
> And it will be established for you;
> So light will shine on your ways.

To "make your prayer" means "to construct." You are going to construct your prayers—you are going to decree what God has put on your heart to desire. You are a royal priesthood adorned with a kingly anointing. A king does not ask for anything; a king declares his decrees, because he has that authority, and those in his world rush to see that they are accomplished.

Don't ever think that you are a weak, defeated victim. The weak are instructed to declare their strength: "Let the weak say, 'I am strong'" (Joel 3:10). Never underestimate the strength that resides in you through Christ. You command a power to change the course of your destiny that the great heroes of the Old Testament could only dream of.

Think for a moment how the patriarchs of Israel attempted to change the trajectory of their lives or their nation:

- Jacob wrestled.
- Lot inquired.

- Moses intervened.
- David repented.
- Solomon asked.
- Daniel fasted.

They strove and pled and fought for the right to influence their destiny—a destiny you have been given the privilege to shape simply by giving the word. Make sure that as you take command that you are heading true north by diligently guarding your heart and staying on heaven's course.

> Guard your heart above all else, for it determines the course of your life.
> —Proverbs 4:23, NLT

# CHAPTER SIX

# THE IMPORTANCE
# OF ORDERING YOUR DAY

Dost thou love Life, then do not squander Time,
for that's the Stuff Life is made of.[1]

—Benjamin Franklin

OUR FUTURE COMES ONE DAY AT A TIME—IT IS GOD'S
present to you. Every moment of every day, with every
thought you think and word you speak, you are making a
decision to move either toward greatness or toward obscurity. If you are to make the most of every opportunity you
are given—if you are to become God's vessel of glory and
honor prepared for every good work—you must learn to
harness, and then maximize, the potential of your thoughts
and words. You must create a royal priestly mind-set by
practicing noble thought habits and disciplining your
tongue to speak success-filled words if you are to become
the champion God has created you to be.

You have been given the opportunity to create a
masterpiece of your life. While your thoughts are the
colors you use to paint the background, your words are
the brushes you use to fill in each detail. To make that

painting the beautiful masterpiece God has planned it to be, however, you must be clear on what those colors and details should look like. As you learned in the last chapter, it is God who has pre-created in intimate detail the spectacular tapestry of your life. It is your job to discover what that looks like and weave it into existence. Like a wireless receiver, you can interface with heaven and download that template from the spiritual realm into your real-time life experience.

**You have been given the opportunity to create a masterpiece of your life. While your thoughts are the colors you use to paint the background, your words are the brushes you use to fill in each detail.**

But there is still more to the story. I cannot teach on the mechanics of creativity without teaching on the dynamics of order. Beauty and creativity are products of clarity and organization. We must be intentional and purposeful with how we use all of the resources at our disposal. Ephesians 5:15–17 (AMP) gives us a foundational key regarding this very principle:

> Look carefully then how you walk! Live purposefully and worthily and accurately, not as the unwise and witless, but as wise (sensible, intelligent people), making the very most of the time [buying up each opportunity], because the days are evil. Therefore do not be vague and thoughtless and foolish, but

understanding and firmly grasping what the will of the Lord is.

The key to making the most of every opportunity is to grasp firmly the will of the Lord. This is why it is vitally important to renew your mind continually with the Word of God. You must daily align your thoughts and words with God's. Jesus gave us a fundamental key to successfully commanding our every situation when He told us in John 15:7, "If you abide in Me, and My words abide in you, you will ask what you desire, and it shall be done for you." This is why God instructs us to meditate on "the Word of God, which is effectually at work in you who believe [exercising its superhuman power in those who adhere to and trust in and rely on it]" (1 Thess. 2:13, AMP). God's Word is life and health to those who find it. (See Proverbs 4:20–22.)

## APPLYING WISDOM

One of the wisest things we can do is to live life on purpose. We are told in Scripture to "redeem the time" (Eph. 5:16). We are to be intentional with how we order our days and spend our time. Everyone in the universe has been given the same quantity of time: we all get twenty-four hours per day whether we live in the White House or the ghetto. What we do with those twenty-four hours determines what we accomplish in our lifetime. I once heard it said that time is God's way of keeping everything from happening at once. We must all learn the art of ordering our day.

In Psalm 90:12, Moses made this request: "Teach us to number our days, that we may gain a heart of wisdom." We are to take into account each day and not squander the time that we have. Wisdom redeems the time and makes the most of every opportunity. We have all heard Benjamin Franklin's famous quip, "Early to Bed, early to rise, makes a Man healthy, wealthy, and wise."[2] It seems simple, but seemingly innocuous time-wasters are one of the enemy's most effective tools in keeping the body of Christ "off task." In an age of time-saving, modern conveniences such as automatic dishwashers and microwave ovens, we also have major "time-depleters" such as television and the Internet. What would Ben Franklin have thought about the masses who stay up watching cable TV until all hours of the night, channel surfing from one infomercial to another because they are too tired to go to bed?

Ordering your day requires the ability to prioritize. It requires the ability to discern what is distracting busywork and what is kingdom business. Effective time management requires getting God's heart on what is

> Everyone in the universe has been given the same quantity of time: we all get twenty-four hours per day whether we live in the White House or the ghetto.

worth "investing" time in versus what we should not be "spending" or even "wasting" time on. As with any financial investment, you must ask what kind of return your time investments are yielding. Time "spent" is a cost—and you must be mindful of the benefit you are exchanging for the cost you are incurring.

## GOD IS A GOD OF ORDER

We experience that God is a God of order by the consistency of seasons, tides, and solar orbits. We can order our lives because we know with what accuracy the sun will set and rise again; how the seasons will change, the tides will turn, and the planets will rotate on their axes. There is a cadence and rhythm to our lives because of the order God has put into place through the universe in which we are suspended and the nature within which we dwell. From ecosystems to solar systems, God has set into motion patterns that we can study and document through what we call science.

God provided the ultimate example of effective time management and order in the Book of Genesis. In six days He created the earth and everything in it, and on the seventh day He rested. It all went according to plan. There was an order to when and how He created what and when—a succession and progression to how He developed each organism and species. God did not waste His resources, especially His time. He was purposeful and concise as He unfolded life on our planet.

Look at Noah, Joseph, Moses, and David. All were men of honor and order. They were disciplined and dedicated, and they submitted themselves to God's commands. They were bold and courageous because they understood the power of a divine hierarchy and authority. They followed orders, knowing the power available in submitting to God. Even Solomon understood the importance of order when he meticulously followed God's instructions and chain of command in building the temple. We read in 2 Chronicles 8:16, "Now all the work of Solomon was well-ordered from the day of the foundation of the house of the LORD until it was finished." In the New Testament, we are urged by Paul regarding God's church to "be sure that everything is done properly and in order" (1 Cor. 14:40, NLT).

Order is a condition in which freedom from disorder or disruption is maintained through structures, systems, and protocol. Whenever there is a lack of order, rank, or command chain; whenever protocol is not present; or whenever a code of conduct is not perceived or understood, it brings about emptiness, lack of purpose, and meaning. If your life is characterized by confusion, conflict, frustration, or lack of direction, meaning, or insight, it is an indication that you are deficient in the area of order. Where there is no order, there is no light:

> A land as dark as darkness itself,
> As the shadow of death, without any order,

Where even the light is like darkness.

—Job 10:22

Until you decide to reverse the perpetual cycle of disorder, you will continue to experience cycles of defeat and failure. This principle is illustrated by the law of entropy—the tendency of energy to dissipate and go from a state of order to one of disorder. Entropy can be defined as a dispersal of energy. Unless you intentionally harness time and energy, unless you command it with the authority you have been given, your life will dissolve into a state of chaos—and you will never experience the life of significance and fruitfulness God has purposed for you. Don't just let things happen; make things happen.

## TAKE CONTROL OF YOUR DAY

Do not miss out on the rewards of well-managed time. Order is what gives you the freedom to be creative. Order gives you the peace of mind you need to tune into God's supernatural frequencies and tap into divine inspiration. Without order you will be distracted with the cares and concerns of this life so that you cannot still your mind to hear God's voice. It is impossible to imagine and envision when you are overextended and stressed. You need to schedule time to purposefully paint the canvas of your life by investing in creative dreaming. Stop to think. Order your day so that you have the time and peace you need to create the masterpiece God has preordained for you.

Like any professional composer, artist, architect, writer, or programmer, you must schedule time to think things through. Form follows thought, and the shape of your life is a product of that thought. Structure your time so that you can structure your thoughts, for they provide the structure for your life. Know when to take hold of an idea and run with it and when to wait and let it mature until it has ripened. Get God's timing. Discern God's order.

A farmer diligently prepares his field, tills the soil in neat rows, and plants his seed in straight lines according to its kind. He knows what he has planted, and he continues to till and cultivate, prune and fertilize, until the harvest is ready. Even in harvesting a bountiful crop, he must be mindful, or he will destroy what he has worked so hard to grow. To maximize the yield of his labor, he carefully gathers, bundles, and stores his produce. Although God gives the increase, we must continually watch over what we have planted to protect it and harvest it at just the right time. Do not underestimate the importance and rewards of doing all things mindfully and in order. It is how we achieve excellence and become people of virtue. Honor and order are closely related. If you order your conduct aright, God will delight in you and show you His salvation. Conversely, if you delight in the Lord, He will order your steps.

To him who orders his conduct aright I will show
the salvation of God.

—Psalm 50:23

The steps of a good man are ordered by the LORD,
and He delights in his way.

—Psalm 37:23

The rewards of order are many. It may seem like a
daunting if not exhausting task to establish a greater
degree of order in your life. That may feel impossible if you
feel you are already overstretched. But taking time to order
your day should not be an additional burden or one more
"to do" on your list of duties and responsibilities. Order
will ease your load and free your mind for greater peace,
joy, and creativity. Take a look at this short list of benefits
you will reap by more effectively ordering your day:

- Sense of control
- Sense of purpose
- Increase in productivity
- An environment of creativity
- Greater focus and flow of accomplishments
- Strength to overcome those little foxes that
  spoil the vine (Song of Sol. 2:15)

## CULTIVATING CLARITY

You may be looking at your life and wondering if it is
possible to remove the cloud of chaos that seems to hold

dominion over you. There are two simple things you can do in order to move toward clearer skies. First, unclutter your environment. Whether at home or at the office, tidy up your immediate surroundings. When you have cleared off your desk or straightened your bedroom, wherever you find yourself, stop for a moment and unclutter your mind. Pause and still your thoughts so you can gain clarity on what is the most important thing for you to focus upon in your present moment.

**Learn to love the dawn, for there is power in the rising of the Son!**

Don't wait until every area of your external environment is completely organized, but create pockets of order where you can clear your mind and order your thoughts. Your immediate environment and the atmospheres you create will go far to enhance the order you are able to establish in your sphere of influence. Practice clearing your head by journaling or meditating on Scripture. Find a space where you can usher in the peace of God by quieting your mind through worship. Dump the distractions that try and push their way into your inner sanctuary by making lists and putting plans on paper to do later. Corral all those rogue thoughts onto a piece of paper where they can remain until you are ready to address them.

When you are ready, cast each care on the Lord one by one, knowing that God is hearing your prayers and watching over His Word to perform it. Jesus said, "And whatever you ask in My name, that I will do, that the Father may be glorified in the Son. If you ask anything in My name, I will do it" (John 14:13–14). And John encouraged us by writing, "Now this is the confidence that we have in Him, that if we ask anything according to His will, He hears us. And if we know that He hears us, whatever we ask, we know that we have the petitions that we have asked of Him" (1 John 5:14–15).

Be still and know that He is God. (See Psalm 46:10.) Focus on doing what you know you should be doing, and let God do His part without doubting if He will or not.

## ORDER COMES EARLY

God is an early riser. The Bible is full of references of His prophets and saints rising early to pray or hear God's voice. God is notorious for waking His followers early in the morning to give them instructions, insights, or warnings. Those who seek to be used of God must be willing to rise up early. Soldiers are ever alert and ready to respond to orders. The bugle blows early because battles are won through the preparations done in the early hours of the day—especially spiritual battles. Learn to love the dawn, for there is power in the rising of the Son!

However, praying early does not only refer to the hour of a day, but it also refers to praying far in advance of something happening—before a situation escalates beyond your control. Part of praying proactively rather than reactively is praying early.

Throughout the Old and New Testaments, we are given lessons on the importance of praying early. Praying early is a kingdom principle. Listen to how the Lord rebuked Jeremiah: "I spoke to you, rising up early and speaking, but you did not hear, and I called you, but you did not answer" (Jer. 7:13). We are told in Matthew 20:1, "For the kingdom of heaven is like a landowner who went out early in the morning to hire laborers for his vineyard."

In Isaiah we read:

> He wakes me up in the morning, wakes me up,
> opens my ears to listen as one ready to take orders.
> —Isaiah 50:4–5, THE MESSAGE

God, the Master Strategist, empowered Moses early in the morning. An effective offense asserts itself early, so God instructed Moses to "rise early in the morning and stand before Pharaoh, and say to him, 'Thus says the LORD God of the Hebrews: "Let My people go, that they may serve Me"'" (Exod. 9:13). And then in Exodus 24:4 we read:

> And Moses wrote all the words of the LORD. And he rose early in the morning, and built an altar at the foot of the mountain, and twelve pillars according to the twelve tribes of Israel.

God speaks through and to His servants early.

In 2 Chronicles, God promises the Israelites victory against their enemies. He tells them not to be afraid of the great multitudes, for He will fight the battle for them. He instructs the Israelites to position themselves and to stand firm. The Lord says to them, "Do not fear or be dismayed; tomorrow go out against them, for the LORD is with you" (2 Chron. 20:17).

> So they rose early in the morning and went out into the Wilderness of Tekoa; and as they went out, Jehoshaphat stood and said, "Hear me, O Judah and you inhabitants of Jerusalem: Believe in the LORD your God, and you shall be established; believe His prophets, and you shall prosper."
> —2 Chronicles 20:20

They rose early and began to sing and praise the Lord. As they sang praises to God, the Lord caused confusion among the enemy camp, and their foes turned on each other until all of them were utterly destroyed. The Israelites spent the next three days carrying away the spoil that was left behind.

Good things come to those who rise early and praise God.

Listen to the words of God's champion, David:

> Awake, my glory!
> Awake, lute and harp!

I will awaken the dawn.

—Psalm 57:8

O God, You are my God;
Early will I seek You.

—Psalm 63:1

The Lord said that David was a man after His own heart. The Bible records that David was Israel's greatest warrior, king, poet, and prophet. He was one of Scripture's most passionate and purposeful characters, and he left an enduring legacy of victory, wisdom, and significance. What set David apart? What caused David to become an enduring hero of the faith? He rose early to seek the Lord.

But David wasn't the only beloved of God to rise early. Jesus, in whom God said He was well pleased, habitually rose early to pray: "Now in the morning, having risen a long while before daylight, He went out and departed to a solitary place; and there He prayed" (Mark 1:35). If the Lord Jesus Christ had to rise early to pray, how much more should we begin our day in prayer?

The very first Christians, who were taught by Christ Himself, rose early to hear the Word of God. In Luke 21:38 we read, "Early in the morning all the people came to Him in the temple to hear Him." And in John 8:2 we read, "At dawn he appeared again in the temple courts, where all the people gathered around him, and he sat down to teach them" (NIV).

This practice continued through to the early church. After they were imprisoned, an angel of the Lord instructed the apostles, "'Go, stand in the temple and speak to the people all the words of this life.' And when they heard that, they entered the temple early in the morning and taught" (Acts 5:20–21).

God wants to give you a prophetic jump-start to your day. Listen to the yearning of God's heart in Jeremiah 35:14–15:

> Although I have spoken to you, rising early and speaking, you did not obey Me. I have also sent to you all My servants the prophets, rising up early and sending them, saying, "Turn now everyone from his evil way, amend your doings, and do not go after other gods to serve them; then you will dwell in the land which I have given you and your fathers." But you have not inclined your ear, nor obeyed Me.

And listen to this warning found in 1 Chronicles:

> The LORD our God broke out against us, because we did not consult Him about the proper order.
> —1 Chronicles 15:13

Getting God's order for every area of our lives is serious business. We serve a God of order. The enemy uses disorder and confusion to wreak destruction. God calls you to follow after peace and righteousness to establish order and freedom. Take dominion over your day, your environment, and your destiny by setting things in their proper order.

Seek the Lord early and consult Him about ordering your day aright!

## RISE EARLY AND COMMAND YOUR MORNING

An important part of ordering your day is rising early to seek the Lord. God wants to speak into your life so that He can help you order your day with greater authority and success. Tap into God's best will for you by rising early to spend time in His presence. Let the Lord fill your heart with His peace and joy, stand firm on His promises, and get His special word for you so that you can stand and declare it throughout the day. Seek wisdom; seek understanding; study to show yourself approved. Rise early, as did the prophet Isaiah, so that you will have the tongue of the wise, ready to give an answer for the hope that is in you.

> Yes, by my spirit within me I will seek You early;
> For when Your judgments are in the earth,
> The inhabitants of the world will learn righteousness.
> —Isaiah 26:9

CHAPTER SEVEN

# HOW TO BECOME
# AN OVERNIGHT SUCCESS

To perceive the world differently, we must be willing
to change our belief system, let the past slip away,
expand our sense of now, and dissolve the fear in
our minds.[1]

—William James

SUCCESS REQUIRES COURAGE AND BOLDNESS. It requires that you walk in genuine spiritual authority in order to take dominion over your inner and outer world. God has empowered you, through Christ, to speak light into every situation. He has given you the tools and ability to dispel the dark and create beauty and order wherever you are. Begin to consider the chaos and formlessness you encounter as a blank canvas upon which you can sketch, or raw clay with which you can mold your dream. Michelangelo's *David*, one of the greatest pieces of art of all time, was just a block of marble like any other before Michelangelo set his hand and chisel to it. Whatever lies before you can

95

be the substance from which you call forth your own masterpiece.

When God dreamed of creation, He spoke into a situation that was dark and "without form." Where there was darkness, God declared light. We read in Genesis 1:2–4 that "the earth was without form, and void; and darkness was upon the face of the deep....Then God said, 'Let there be light'; and there was light...and God divided the light from the darkness." God created paradise and then gave His ultimate creation, man, the authority to rule over it. He told Adam to name every creature, calling each one out before him one at a time—thus Adam proclaimed the name of and ordered every species. Man was given dominion over all creation and the power to silence all of his enemies. (See Psalm 8.) God didn't create mankind to be idle but to be an active participant in making the earth over into the form God intended. God locked up all the mysteries of what humanity would ever need in what He created, so that we could co-labor with Him to unravel those mysteries and continue moving creation toward its expected end.

## LEARNING TO REIGN IN GLORY

Jesus spoke many parables so that His disciples could conceptualize the power at their disposal and learn to operate successfully in His kingdom. He wanted them to comprehend the degree of success and prosperity that was available to them if they pursued these kingdom principles.

When I speak of success and prosperity, I am speaking of these concepts from the context of the kingdom. Success is the fulfillment of divine purpose, while prosperity is having enough divine provision to overcome obstacles. Once you press out of one situation, realm, or domain, you will rise to a new level of strength with a greater capacity to influence your new situation or domain. In other words, you will go from one glory to another and from one level of strength to a greater one. When you learn to build on your experiences, adding to your faith, you will live a successful kingdom life as ambassadors of God's glorious kingdom. You will progress from one level of success and provision to another as you develop godly ability and character. Listen to how Peter admonished early believers:

> But also for this very reason, giving all diligence, add to your faith virtue, to virtue knowledge, to knowledge self-control, to self-control perseverance, to perseverance godliness, to godliness brotherly kindness, and to brotherly kindness love. For if these things are yours and abound, you will be neither barren nor unfruitful in the knowledge of our Lord Jesus Christ.
>
> —2 Peter 1:5–8

When Peter says "for this very reason," he is referring to having been called to partake of God's divine nature (v. 4). As an ambassador, you are called to represent your heavenly Father in the earthly realm. You are to "re-present" Him, or "present Him again," in every avenue of secular interaction. The world has formulated an erroneous and limited concept of God, and you are called to demonstrate His greatness through your lifestyle. God has called you to be His showcase on the earth—everything about you should reflect the glories of the kingdom, from the clothes you wear to the way you talk—everything that speaks to your station and quality of life—all should demonstrate the limitless glories of the kingdom of God!

**Success is the fulfillment of divine purpose, while prosperity is having enough divine provision to overcome obstacles.**

You are also called to bring the systems of this world into divine alignment. First Peter 2:9 tells us that we are kingly priests: "a royal priesthood, a holy nation, His own special people, that you may proclaim the praises of Him who called you out of darkness into His marvelous light." Your priestly anointing empowers you to worship and offer sacrifices of praise to God. Your kingly anointing gives you the power and authority to legislate, regulate, enforce, and establish—to reign, rule, and dominate. As a believer, you must understand that you have become privy to the mystery of these kingdom principles or keys so that in this life you can walk in divine dominion. "And I will give you the keys of the kingdom of heaven, and whatever you bind on earth will be bound in heaven, and whatever you loose on earth will be loosed in heaven" (Matt. 16:19). In other words, whatever you allow in the earthly realm, heaven allows, and whatever you say no to in Jesus's name, heaven will back you up by binding it. Remember, nothing leaves heaven until the request for it leaves Earth. This is how powerful the spoken word is. It has the ability to open or close spiritual and heavenly portals.

God set this principle in place when He declared through Isaiah:

> So shall My word be that goes forth from My mouth; it shall not return to Me void, but it shall accomplish what I please, and it shall prosper in the thing for which I sent it.
>
> —Isaiah 55:11

As a living epistle, a carrier of the Spirit of Christ, the Word has been made flesh in you, and the God-breathed words that you speak, as a temple of the living God, carry a supernatural authority and creative power. "Do you not know that you are the temple of God and that the Spirit of God dwells in you?" (1 Cor. 3:16).

Words are powerful. Words affect your destiny. One day

of murmuring and complaining has the power to set you back for a year. That's a 1-to-365-day ratio. Therefore, you can't afford to release capricious words out of your mouth because the spirit realm takes every word uttered from man as a command and mandate. It does not discriminate between a jest, a joke, a desire, an order, or a decree. This is how powerful the spoken word is. Remember what happened in the desert to the children of Israel. Be careful not to become ensnared by your own words.

> A man's belly shall be satisfied with the fruit of his mouth; and with the increase of his lips shall he be filled.
>
> —Proverbs 18:20, KJV

## PRAY STRATEGICALLY

Sometimes your success, your progress, or your blessings can be held up and hindered not because you are speaking negatively, but because others have released negative words over your life and you have accepted them as true. Refuse to sit back and passively let life happen to you. Get actively involved in your own destiny. Aggressively reverse ill-spoken words, hexes, spells, and bad wishes. Proactively design, construct, and engineer your life. What do you want your life to look like next week, next year, or even at your funeral? Will you be remembered for your accomplishments—or only for what you might have done?

According to Jeremiah 29:11, God does not start a thing without knowing the outcome—He begins every work with the end in mind. Since He already knows the end from the beginning, He must know everything in between. Seek His face in prayer. "If any of you lacks wisdom, let him ask of God, who gives to all liberally and without reproach" (James 1:5). Make inquiries concerning the plans He has for you. Discover His will as He speaks to your heart and mind, and then legislate His will in the earthly realm through daily declarations. By your words you establish life or death, blessings or curses, success or failure.

**You can't afford to release capricious words out of your mouth because the spirit realm takes every word uttered from man as a command and mandate....This is how powerful the spoken word is.**

In Matthew 13:52, Jesus states that a person who is coached to participate in the kingdom of heaven is one who is able to tap into both ancient truth and fresh wisdom. Let's look at how the Amplified Bible interprets this verse of Scripture:

> He said to them, Therefore every teacher and interpreter of the Sacred Writings who has been

instructed about and trained for the kingdom of
heaven and has become a disciple is like a house-
holder who brings forth out of his storehouse
treasure that is new and [treasure that is] old [the
fresh as well as the familiar].

In other words, we seek insight and guidance for
prayer from both the Old and the New Testament.
Prayer is a time-honored kingdom discipline. It is the
means by which we communicate with God, and it is
how God communicates with us. Your prayers should
be constructed in such a manner that they issue forth
from the living Word of God, incorporating both established principles as well as fresh revelation. To keep your
prayer life vibrant and exciting, you should use a variety
of strategies as well as a diversity of goals.

## TAKE COMMAND IN ADVANCE: THE IMPORTANCE OF KEEPING WATCH

Becoming an "overnight success" will only happen after
you have successfully ordered your thoughts, words, and
time. All of these components working together will
empower you with the prayer strategy I call "Commanding
Your Morning." What I want to convey here, particularly,
is that in this context, morning does not solely refer to the
hours registered on the face of a clock but to the period
of time that exists before circumstances happen. You do

not have to wait to get sick or experience financial loss or plummeting marriage relations before positioning and posturing yourself to pray. There are many occurrences in your life that are the work of the enemy and can be prohibited through preemptive prayer.

In the New Testament, we read of a specific prayer strategy Jesus employed. Let's look at Matthew 14:23–32:

> And when He had sent the multitudes away, He went up on the mountain by Himself to pray. Now when evening came, He was alone there. But the boat was now in the middle of the sea, tossed by the waves, for the wind was contrary. Now in the fourth watch of the night Jesus went to them, walking on the sea. And when the disciples saw Him walking on the sea, they were troubled, saying, "It is a ghost!" And they cried out for fear. But immediately Jesus spoke to them, saying, "Be of good cheer! It is I; do not be afraid." And Peter answered Him and said, "Lord, if it is You, command me to come to You on the water." So He said, "Come." And when Peter had come down out of the boat, he walked on the water to go to Jesus. But when he saw that the wind was boisterous, he was afraid; and beginning to sink he cried out, saying, "Lord, save me!" And immediately Jesus stretched out His hand and caught him, and said to him, "O you of little faith, why did you doubt?" And when they got into the boat, the wind ceased.

In the above text, Jesus teaches us how to gain control over our day so that we dethrone evil from its place of power. The strategy you are about to embark on is particularly useful during times of transition. Transition requires a change in how we pray because the natural man cannot understand the things of God. In transition you must seek the counsel of God, not the counsel of man. Also, you must be careful not to embrace the counsel of debilitating spirits such as fear, doubt, and unbelief. For he who sooner or later advances in life through prayer will inevitably be greeted in his future by the intoxicating aromas of divine success, supernatural accomplishments, and continuous moments of heavenly bliss, peace, and contentment.

Jesus had already prayed from ten to twelve hours before He got His release. He was using a specific prayer strategy that I have called "Commanding the Morning." Long before the enemy manifested himself by devising a storm, Jesus had programmed life, prosperity, and success into His day and into the lives of His disciples. The devil could not kill them or cause them to fail. Although they met with frustrating circumstances, they prevailed because Jesus had already paved the way to their success with His prayers.

This principle can be found in the Old Testament as well. Job 38:12–13 reveals a conversation God had with

Job. He asked a series of questions that exposes the principle of commanding the morning:

> Have you commanded the morning since your
>    days began,
> And caused the dawn to know its place,
> That it might take hold of the ends of the earth,
> And the wicked be shaken out of it?

God asked Job, "Have you commanded the morning?" Long before the average believer has awakened to even consider their day, witches and warlocks have been diligently perched upon their posts releasing spells and hexes. The witching hour is the time when supernatural creatures such as witches, demons, and ghosts are at their most powerful and black magic is most effective. They consider the midnight hour to be the greatest time to effect change and transformation in the spiritual realm.

By the time we Christians arise for what we call "early morning prayer," which is usually somewhere between 4:00 a.m. and 6:00 a.m., those who work with the dark art of divination have completed their diabolical assignments, and the satanic sabotage of your day has already been set in motion. Many Christians have become discouraged simply because they have prayed amiss—they missed the time of declaration and neglected to command their morning.

This divine principle is taken from Genesis, chapter

1, where it is written: "And the evening and the morning was the first...second...third...fourth...fifth...sixth day." God actually worked from the evening to the morning, rather from morning to evening.

During Jesus's generation, a watch constituted a three-hour period. The first watch would begin at 6:00 p.m., the second at 9:00 p.m., the third at midnight, the fourth at 3:00 a.m., and the fifth at 6:00 a.m. There would be a total of eight watches, four in the night and four in the day. If you are a mathematician, you have probably concluded that eight watches constitute a twenty-four-hour day.

Therefore, those early hours of prayer should be placed within the context of the evening to morning watches, which actually begin at 6:00 p.m. and end at 6:00 a.m. It is important to understand that the ending of a watch shift is just as important as the beginning, because it is during this time frame that the enemy will attempt to set up an ambush and attack. According to 1 Peter 5:8, you must "be sober, be vigilant; because your adversary the devil walks about like a roaring lion, seeking whom he may devour."

If you are assigned to the last two watches of the night—midnight to 3:00 a.m. and 3:00 a.m. to 6:00 a.m.—your role is an important one because you are standing in the gap to reinforce the prayer hedges that have been established in preceding watches. Remember, the last watch is more effective if those assigned to it understand the context of the entire night watch vigil.

Every effort should be made to reinforce a prayer agenda that is embraced by all watches.

As the Chief Intercessor, Jesus knew the most effective time to pray. He was God in action, and He deemed it as a divine imperative to begin His prayer watch sometime during the first watch, which was approximately 6:00 p.m. As a prayer general, Jesus was an adept prayer technician able to pray with fluency, proficiency, clarity, and accuracy for as long as it was necessary to pray for something. I pray that God will grant you the same divine ability.

## APPLYING THE DISCIPLINE
## OF KINGDOM LIVING

After a period of successful ministry, Jesus orchestrated a new object lesson for His disciples. He wanted to expose them to the discipline of kingdom living—for kingdom living demands disciplined effort, strategic prayer, and divine awareness. Prior to every great kingdom event demonstrated by Jesus, the Bible indicates that He spent a minimum of ten to twelve hours in prayer. Jesus was establishing God's divine agenda in the earth realm and downloading victory, success, and prosperity into His day while dislodging evil. He was commanding the morning and taking authority over His day. To command means to:

- Instruct
- Dictate

- Exercise authority
- Master and conquer
- Control
- Give orders to
- Demand so as to receive what is due
- Rule
- Decree
- Supervise
- Keep watch
- Manage
- Administrate
- Regulate

Don't miss this principle. The power for change is in your mouth. The power for prosperity is in your mouth. The power for health and healing is in your mouth. The power for a successful ministry, marriage, business, relationship, or whatever you need is in your mouth!

When you command your morning, you pull success from the spiritual realm into your day. When you command your morning, you give your reality divine assignments. You must be willing to declare and establish in the spirit realm today what you want to see manifested tomorrow. When you understand and implement this prayer strategy, you will literally begin to experience what I call "overnight" success. When I say "overnight" I am referring once again to the power of the spoken word in relation to God's eternal plan for your life and your prayer posture relative to setting these plans into motion. What you decree forth before you go to bed at night and continue to declare as you rise in the morning will keep the spiritual world active all night long—while you sleep the peaceful sleep of the righteous!

God's plans are to bless and not to curse; to make alive and not kill; to prosper you and not cause you to fail. Praying during the night causes your morning to be bright and to abound with goodness. You will start your day with power and end it with blessing. Remember, when we refer to days, nights, and seasons, we are not referring to the time on a clock or a day on a calendar; we are referring to the timing of the Lord, which requires neither a clock nor a calendar. His timing for blessing is now, in the present moment, and is regulated by simple and continual acts of obedience. (See Deuteronomy 28:1–2.)

According to Isaiah 1:19, "If you are willing and obedient, you shall eat the good of the land." Are you willing?

When you employ this strategy, you activate the twenty-four-hour anointing—an anointing that brings all the elements surrounding your life into divine alignment with God's purpose for you. This anointing brings you to a kind of prophetic critical mass. An example of this would be the life of Joseph. One night after a long period of captivity,

> **God's plans are to bless and not to curse; to make alive and not kill; to prosper you and not cause you to fail.**

Joseph went to bed a felon, and he woke up positioned to be prime minister. All the elements of his life collided with purpose and exploded into a prophetic critical mass. There was nothing and no one that could stop his impending success and prosperity. When you command your morning, nothing and no one can hinder, alter, or abort your destiny.

> Then let him declare it and set it in order for Me…
> And the things that are coming and shall come,
> Let them show these to them.
> —Isaiah 44:7

## Chapter Eight

# COMMANDING
# YOUR MORNING

O while I live to be the ruler of life, not a slave,
To meet life as a powerful conqueror…
And nothing exterior to me will ever take
    command of me.[1]

—Walt Whitman

AN WAS CREATED IN THE IMAGE OF GOD AND
after His likeness. He was then given a mandate
to rule and to dominate his world. He was given the delegated authority to preside over the earth and to protect it from negative forces that could create disequilibrium, distress, destitution, and disease.

God said in the Book of Job that you shall decree a thing and it shall be established (Job 22:28). Your miracle already exists in the unseen "secret" realm. All secret things belong to God, but those things that are revealed belong to man. In Proverbs 25:2 (NLT) we read, "It is God's privilege to conceal things and the king's privilege to discover them." Solomon also put it this way:

> I set my heart to seek and search out by wisdom concerning all that is done under heaven; this burdensome task God has given to the sons of man, by which they may be exercised.
>
> —Ecclesiastes 1:13

## IN SEARCH OF WISDOM

It is at the point of revelation—or divine inspiration—that God speaks to us all. He said, "'For I know the plans I have for you,' declares the LORD, 'plans to prosper you and not to harm you, plans to give you hope and a future'" (Jer. 29:11, NIV). He knows the end from the beginning and everything in between. And these are the things that He wants to reveal to you. The Book of Job says that this is what God actually does; He opens up the mind of man and speaks inspirational thoughts so that He can keep man from pursuing his own limited way. God's thoughts are of abundance and not lack—He wants you to live large and to bring you into a good life. He gives you divine inspirational thoughts and the ability to speak them into existence so that you will grow to fulfill His best plan for your life. He wants you to mature in wisdom, authority, and supernatural ability so that you can bear witness to the splendor of His kingdom. Your miracle is already in existence, but it is up to you to learn to see it and to call it out.

## TAKE COMMAND
## BY MAKING THE CALL

In Matthew 21:2, when Jesus was preparing for His final entry into Jerusalem, He called for a donkey to be brought to Him, but the donkey stayed tied up until Jesus called for it. Likewise, the thing you need might already by waiting for you, but you don't see it yet because you have not yet called for it. A situation or circumstance generally comes because you have called it to you—you have given it permission to exist in your life. Casual words that on the surface may feel as though they are spoken out of humility—as though they are politely self-deprecating, politically correct, or "not overly optimistic"—can do more harm than you think. Remember, whatever you bind or loose on the earth will be bound or loosed in heaven—and that the Lord said, "Just as you have spoken in My hearing, so I will do to you" (Num. 14:28).

Throughout the Bible God is calling His people to take command of their destinies by learning to command their mornings. Command means "to order with authority; to take charge of; to exercise direct authority over; to lead; to dominate by position; to guard; to overlook." Don't let your day get the best of you by not commanding the best from your day. Take command of your thoughts, words, and time so that you will be in a position to take command of your destiny. "Keep awake! Do not sleep like others. Watch and keep your minds awake to what is happening" (1 Thess. 5:6, NLV). ⁑

Do not be a victim. Call the shots and change your destiny. Be proactive and decisive as you declare God's Word over your life. God has given you the promise that whatsoever you declare in Jesus's name, it will be done (John 14:13–14), so you can be all He intended you to be on the earth—a shining example of God's goodness and love.

> Set your words in order before me; take your stand.
> —Job 33:5

> Stand your ground.... Stay alert and be persistent in your prayers.
> —Ephesians 6:14, 18, NLT

## DECREE AND DECLARE PROSPECTIVELY

There should be no doubt in your mind that God wants to bless and prosper you. He wants you to succeed and not fail. He wants the very best for you. Remember, those that come to God must believe that He rewards those who diligently seek Him (Heb. 11:6). This is because the one thing that pleases God is your faith. Furthermore, let your declarations be informed by the following revolutionary—and "revelationary"—truth:

Now salvation, and strength, and the kingdom of our God, and the power of His Christ have come, for the accuser of our brethren, who accused them before our God day and night, has been cast down. And they overcame him by the blood of the Lamb and by the word of their testimony.

—Revelation 12:10–11

Amen!

Your enemy is overcome by the blood of the Lamb and the word of your testimony. You must declare, "He who is in [me] is greater than he who is in the world" (1 John 4:4), and "In all these things we are more than conquerors through Him who loved us" (Rom. 8:37). Believe and confess: "For with the heart one believes unto righteousness, and with the mouth confession is made unto salvation" (Rom. 10:10). Speak with conviction and confess with expectation.

**Ask the Holy Spirit to guide your words, thoughts, and faith as you take command of your day.**

Expect that whatever you are decreeing will come to pass. Jesus taught in Mark 11:24, "Whatever things you ask when you pray, believe that you receive them, and you will have them." Yet in the same verse, Jesus emphasized the need for us to "speak" and "say" three times more than He did "believe." Since the spirit realm is the causal realm, expect that whatever you are praying will manifest on this side of glory because it has already been sealed in the spirit realm. God has already released every possibility before the foundation of the world. Do not be counterproductive in your declarations by decreeing one thing and confessing the other. Be consistent in knowing that when you commit to the releasing of those things that pertain to your life, God is saying that whatsoever (positive or negative, faith or unbelief) you loose is loosed, and whatsoever you bind is bound. Remember, as soon as a declaration leaves your mouth, it has already happened.

> You will also declare a thing,
> And it will be established for you;
> So light will shine on your ways.
>
> —Job 22:28

## DECLARE AND DECREE AUTHORITATIVELY

Make your declaration in Jesus's name. God delegated authority to you, as a believer, that you may accomplish His will on the earth. Inherent within this divine authority is the mantle of responsibility and accountability. You are responsible to speak in accordance with the divine will that has been spoken concerning you. Kingdom authority demands that you become proactive in the establishment of purpose in your life experience. You are not to be dominated by circumstances—you are to take authority over them and decree the will of

God into manifestation in the name of Jesus. "I tell you the truth, my Father will give you whatever you ask in my name" (John 16:23, NIV).

> Now to Him Who, by (in consequence of) the [action of His] power that is at work within us, is able to [carry out His purpose and] do super-abundantly, far over and above all that we [dare] ask or think [infinitely beyond our highest prayers, desires, thoughts, hopes, or dreams]—to Him be glory in the church and in Christ Jesus throughout all generations forever and ever. Amen (so be it).
>
> —Ephesians 3:20–21, AMP

## THE POWER OF PRAYER-WALKING

I have personally integrated the declarations contained in this book into my daily exercise routine. I need to exercise to maintain my health and I love to walk, so I accomplish two life-sustaining essentials with one activity. This practice not only promotes physical strength, stamina, and overall health, but it also builds strong prayer muscles, increasing spiritual stamina and fortitude. Think about "walking in the Spirit" as you walk out your destiny with your words. Practice keeping step with the Spirit as you declare His promises over your life. Galatians 5:25 states, "Since we live by the Spirit, let us keep in step with the Spirit" (NIV). Amen

Develop the habit of prayer-walking. As you walk, think about God's promise to enlarge your territory and give you every place you set your foot. As you walk, release these powerful declarations into the atmosphere for three consecutive months, and watch what God will do. He is getting ready to blow your mind with blessings. He will reverse negative circumstances. He will position you for supernatural abundance and unprecedented favor. Without a shadow of doubt, He will show up mighty on your behalf. Your breakthrough and miracles are on the way!

## PUTTING IT INTO PRACTICE

I have included a list of activation declarations that you can use during your time of prayer. This is not meant to become a binding religious practice or ritual but as a guideline and framework to launch you into the practice of commanding your morning. As you speak out these declarations, do so boldly but also prayerfully. Ask the Holy Spirit to guide your words, thoughts, and faith as you take command of your day. Every reader's situation is unique, and only you know what your specific needs are. This is a guide to expand your understanding of what is possible and to get you started; as you step out in faith, the Holy Spirit will lead you into other areas He would have you exercise your authority over.

As you read through the declarations, don't merely read them; speak them aloud with faith, authority, and power. Remember, you are partnering with God to activate His perfect will for you in this life. You are co-laboring with Christ on your own behalf as well as on the behalf of those you are praying for. Let today be the unveiling of a fresh anointing in your life! Let today be the day that you apprehend the power that God has allotted for you! Make the activation declarations a vivid part of your prayer routine, and watch God turn things around! You are on your way to kingdom success and prosperity!

## ACTIVATION DECLARATIONS

**I stand to command my morning and declare it is a new day.**

I take authority over my day in the name of Jesus. Every element of my day shall cooperate with purpose and destiny.

Today is the dawning of a new day. My season of frustration and failures is over, and I walk in a season of success and prosperity. Old things have passed away; all things have become new.

Today I press toward the mark of the high calling of God in Christ Jesus.

Anything or anyone assigned to undermine, frustrate, hinder, or hurt me, I command to be moved out of my sphere of influence in Jesus's name.

I command my day to fully cooperate with Your plan and purpose for it.

I greet today with great anticipation of the good things You have prepared for me.

I decree and declare that a new day is dawning for my ministry and job or business, for my finances, for my relationships, and for my health.

I download success, prosperity, health, wealth, vision, direction, ingenuity, creativity, spirituality, holiness, righteousness, peace, and resourcefulness from Your Spirit into my day.

I have a fresh excitement.

I have a fresh mind.

I have a fresh zeal.

I have a fresh anointing that is uncontaminated and uncompromised.

By this anointing, every yoke is broken off my life and is destroyed; every burden is lifted. His yoke is easy and His burden is light.

**All-powerful God, place Your anointing upon me.**

The anointing that is on my life repels every individual with a diabolical assignment.

Let the anointing flow uncontaminated and unhindered upon my life.

The anointing that is on my life for this season, mission, mandate, and purpose attracts only those with divinely ordained assignments.

Place the following anointings upon me:

- Solomon's anointing for resource management, wisdom, wealth, success, and prosperity

- Isaac's anointing for investment strategies

- Cyrus's anointing for financial acumen

- Samuel's anointing for sensitivity and obedience to the voice of God

- Esther's anointing for divine favor and kingdom strategies

- Daniel's anointing for government, excellence, and integrity

- Joseph's anointing for political, business, and economic leadership strategies

- Joshua's anointing for warfare prosperity and success strategies

- Abraham's anointing for pioneering new territories, real estate acquisitions, and intergenerational covenant blessings

- Moses's anointing as a trailblazer and leader

- Nehemiah's anointing as a renovator and restorer

- Ezra's anointing as an authentic worshiper of the true and living God

- Deborah's anointing for balance

- David's anointing for worship and praise

- Paul's anointing for cutting-edge apostolic revelation
- Elijah's anointing for prophetic accuracy and insights
- Elisha's anointing for servanthood, ministerial succession, and the double portion of jurisdictional power and authority
- Issachar's anointing for the discernment of correct times and seasons
- Abigail's anointing for hospitality and prudence
- Anna's anointing of intercession
- Christ's anointing for prophetic prayer, spiritual warfare, signs, wonders, miracles, and a purpose-driven life
- Uzziah's anointing for technological advancement
- The disciples' anointing for learning
- Jabez's anointing for the territorial and intellectual growth
- Eve's anointing for fruitfulness and dominion

Cause the apostolic and prophetic anointing to converge, explode, and be manifested in my life with accuracy, authenticity, clarity, and elegance.

**Father, I pray:**

"Cause me to hear Your lovingkindness in the morning, for in You do I trust; cause me to know the way in which I should walk, for I lift up my soul to You.... Teach me to do Your will, for You are my God; your Spirit is good. Lead me in the land of uprightness" (Ps. 143:8, 10).

Synchronize my life with Your perfect will, agenda, and calendar.

Superimpose Your will over the will of evil spirits and evil men.

Empower me to serve You in holiness and righteousness.

Grant me divine kingdom asylum and diplomatic immunity from evil that seeks to imprison and entrap me.

Since my times are in Your hands, You will deliver me from the hands of my enemies and from those who persecute me.

Dismantle evil powers working to frustrate my day, assignments, and activities.

Thwart the arrows shot toward me by day and cause the terror by night to cease.

Rescue me from my enemies, for I hide myself in You.

Cause the east winds of judgment to blow into the enemy's camp. Stop the diabolical cyclones and demonic winds designed to bring shipwreck and disaster into my life.

Cause divine and fresh winds of the Holy Spirit to blow. Let the west winds of replenishment, the north winds of abundance, and the south winds of restoration and supernatural supply blow profusely.

Assign angels as my divine escorts and supernatural security. Let them marshal the boundaries and borders of my spheres of influence. Let them dismantle and destroy satanic strongholds and dispossess satanic squatters.

Close the gates of death and seal up the doors of affliction and torment.

Open divine gates of access to new doors of opportunity; windows of divine inspiration, insight, and revelation; paths of righteousness; avenues of success and prosperity; multiple streams of income and positive cash flow; highways to places of divine assignments and prosperity; and channels for transition and deliverance.

Teach me Your way, so that I may know how to conduct my affairs in the most discerning, expeditious, and fiscally wise manner.

Open my eyes to cutting-edge technologies, methodologies, tactics, and strategies that can aid me in doing Your will.

Father, allow only those with divine assignments to be drawn to me.

Let Your Holy Spirit and His wisdom, understanding, counsel, might, knowledge, the fear of the Lord, and prophetic insight be upon me today.

Grant me the ability to hear clearly as You give me insight, witty ideas, and creative inventions.

Open my ears and let Your Word inspire me to righteousness.

Open my ears to the symphonic movements of the Spirit with clear, crisp transmission.

Cause my spiritual eyes to function with 20/20 vision for the correct insight, understanding, and interpretations of the choreographic movements of God.

Let not my eyes be seduced by the spirit of covetousness or my mind by the pride of life.

Make my feet as hinds' feet over all my troubles.

Lead me along the paths of righteousness for Your name's sake.

Holy Spirit, give me new ways of living and better strategies; upgrade me with kingdom technology and kingdom methodology; I receive the supernatural discipline to implement them today.

Father, place the anointing of a warrior upon me. Every domain and system that You have assigned me I confiscate from the enemy. I release the law of dispossession; every satanic or demonic squatter that is on my land, property, or territory, I command to go in the name of Jesus. I am more than a conqueror!

Strengthen the hedge of protection around my life, my possessions, my family, my friends and associates, and my ministry.

Father, I pray all of this on my behalf and on behalf of [include specific names of individuals, organizations, ministries, or families].

You used all Your divine skill to put me together; I am fearfully and wonderfully made.

I remind principalities, powers, and familiar spirits that they have no right to touch my life in any way, for I am in covenant with God and hidden in the secret place of the Most High.

Holy Spirit, lead and guide me into all truth. Order my steps according to Your Word and Your original plan and purpose for my life.

**I release my name into the atmosphere and declare:**

I have a good reputation. There are no negative stigmas attached to me.

I am a campaigner of empowerment. My name is associated with:

- Greatness
- Nobility
- Holiness
- Ethical dealings
- Humility
- Love
- Peace
- Gentleness
- Faith
- Self-control
- Fairness
- Wisdom
- Luxury
- Health
- Prosperity
- Prayer and spiritual warfare
- Kingdom undertakings
- Integrity
- Righteousness
- Morality
- Honesty
- Grace
- Joy
- Long-suffering
- Meekness
- Goodness
- Generosity
- Vision
- Wealth
- Extravagance
- Intelligence
- Knowledge
- The anointing
- Kingdom wisdom
- Success

I release my name and all that is assigned to me and associated with me into the atmosphere. Allow prayer warriors to pick me up in the realm of the spirit and pray, reinforcing my hedge of protection. Let them stand in the prophetic and intercessory gap for me and all that is assigned to me and associated with me.

**In Jesus's name, I reinforce that:**

I am a son of God.

I am saved by grace.

I am born of incorruptible seed.

I am redeemed by the blood.

I am forgiven of all my sins.

I am a new creature in Christ.

I am redeemed from the curse of the law.

I am beloved of God.

I am seated in heavenly places in Christ Jesus.

I am a part of the royal priesthood.

I am a member of a chosen generation.

I am an ambassador for Christ, the light of the world.

I am a citizen of the kingdom of heaven.

I am a joint heir with Jesus.

I am accepted in the Beloved.

I am complete in Him.

I am crucified with Christ.

I am alive with Christ.

I am free from condemnation.

I am reconciled to God.

I am justified by faith.

I am qualified to share in Jesus's inheritance.

I am a fellow citizen with the saints and the household of God.

I am a significant, contributing member of the body of Christ.

I am the temple of the Holy Spirit.

I am the salt of the earth.

I am the bride of Christ.

I am sealed with the Holy Spirit of promise.

I am a saint.

I am the elect of God.

I am established by grace.

I am drawn near to God by the blood of Christ.

I am victorious through Christ.

I am purposely built and uniquely designed for success.

I am set free.

I am a disciple of Christ.

I am a steward of great wealth.

I am a visionary.

I am the head and not the tail.

I am above and not beneath.

I am first and not last.

I am strong in the Lord.

I am more than a conqueror.

I am firmly rooted, built up, and established in the faith.

I am abounding in a spirit of thanksgiving.

I am spiritually circumcised.

I am the righteousness of God.

I am a partaker of His divine nature.

I am an heir according to the promise.

I am called of God.

I am fearfully and wonderfully made.

I am the apple of my Father's eye.

I am healed by the stripes of Jesus Christ.

I am being changed into His image.

I am fathered from above.

I am filled with the Holy Spirit.

I am God's workmanship created in Christ Jesus.

I am delivered from the power of darkness.

I am translated into the kingdom of God.

I am hidden in the secret place of the Most High.

I am defensively clad with the armor of God.

I am offensively equipped with the sword of the Spirit, which is the Word of God.

I am protected by angels.

I am an overcomer.

I am transformed by the renewing of my mind.

I am God's representative in the earth realm.

I am unable to be touched by evil.

I am empowered to successfully engage in spiritual warfare and achieve victory.

I am forgiven of all my sins and redeemed through the blood.

I am blessed with all spiritual blessings in heavenly places.

I am chosen of God, holy and blameless before Him in love.

I am complete in Christ.

I am overtaken with blessings:

- Blessed to achieve national prominence
- Blessed in the city
- Blessed in the field
- Blessed to achieve fruitfulness in all areas
- Blessed in daily provision
- Blessed in daily activities
- Blessed with victory
- Blessed as an entrepreneur
- Blessed socially
- Blessed financially
- Blessed economically
- Blessed corporally
- Blessed commercially
- Blessed relationally
- Blessed interpersonally
- Blessed behaviorally
- Blessed physiologically
- Blessed emotionally
- Blessed spiritually
- Blessed psychologically
- Blessed biochemically
- Blessed neurologically
- Blessed systemically
- Blessed molecularly
- Blessed cellularly
- Blessed skeletally
- Blessed anatomically

- Blessed muscularly
- Blessed hormonally
- Blessed genetically
- Blessed epidermally
- Blessed nutritionally
- Blessed culturally
- Blessed globally
- Blessed educationally
- Blessed technologically

**Almighty God, bless the works of my hand and provide:**

Work opportunities

Advancements

Raises and bonuses

Wisdom and knowledge

Understanding

Assets

Investment strategies

Benefits and promotions

Overtime

Customers and clients

Vision and dreams

Multimillion-dollar ideas, inventions, and strategies

Writing abilities

Best sellers and classics

Theological insights

Innovative goods and world-class services

Sales and commissions

Favorable settlements

Estates and inheritances

Interest and dividends

Multiple streams of income

Profits and bonuses

Rebates and returns

Checks in the mail

Unexpected financial blessings

Wealth transfers

Royalties

Real estate

Secret riches and hidden treasures

Favor with creditors

Increased income

Bills paid

Debts canceled

Supernatural increase and supply

Synergistic relationships

Divine health

Divine networks

Quantum progress

Accelerated growth and development

New ways of living

New ways to work

Strategic positioning

Unexpected gifts

Wonderful surprises

Condominiums and contracts

Automobiles

Debt-free living

Self-sustaining cash flow

Money-management skills

Time-management skills

Mind-management skills

Leadership skills

Effective communication skills

Negotiation skills

Crisis-management skills

Change-management skills

Resource-management skills

Trailblazing skills

Mutually beneficial and synergistic relationships

A kingdom millionaire mind-set:

- I am an underwriter of kingdom initiatives, enterprising activities, and programs.
- I am a kingdom millionaire. I do not only make millions, but I also give millions to worthy kingdom causes and community enrichment.

**Lord, according to Your Word, I declare:**

"Let integrity and uprightness preserve me; for I wait on You" (Ps. 25:21).

"Make me to know my end, and what is the measure of my days, that I may know how frail I am" (Ps. 39:4).

My thoughts are governed only by "things true, noble, reputable, authentic, compelling, gracious—the best, not the worst; the beautiful, not the ugly; things to praise, not things to curse" (Phil. 4:8–9, THE MESSAGE).

"The hand of the diligent shall bear rule" (Prov. 12:24, KJV). I am diligent; therefore, I rule.

By Your stripes I am healed from every physical and emotional wound and illness (according to Isaiah 53:5).

According to Philippians 4:6–7, I speak peace to all anxiety, depression, neurosis, psychosis, fibromyalgia, and chronic pain syndromes; all bipolar, schizophrenic, and schizo-affective disorders; all obsessive-compulsive and post-traumatic stress disorders, and I command their power to be broken from touching my life.

According to Hebrews 10:22, I draw near to You with a true heart in full assurance of faith, having my heart sprinkled from an evil conscience and my body washed with pure water. I speak divine healing and regression of all coronary artery disease and all cerebral vascular disease. The arteries of my heart, brain, and major organs are now washed free of plaque and cholesterol; I am free from the risk of stroke, hardening of the arteries, blindness, hypertension, renal failure, heart attack, angina, and chronic chest pain. I speak supernatural victory over chronic infections and declare healing over meningitis, osteomyelitis, pelvic inflammatory disease, myositis, and all forms of endocarditis.

According to Isaiah 45:17, no weapon formed against me will prosper. I decree and declare victory over all autoimmune disorders and speak healing to all forms of lupus, rheumatoid arthritis, thyroiditis, conjunctivitis, allergic rhinitis, Crohn's disease and ulcerative colitis, diverticulitis, gout, Lyme disease and chronic cellulitis, myocarditis, uveitis, and optic neuritis.

I superimpose the law of the Spirit of life in Christ Jesus over the law of sin and death and decree and declare that I am healed of terminal cancer and tumors, AIDS, seizures, strokes, Parkinson's disease, multiple sclerosis, ALS, emphysema, and sickle cell disease. According to Psalm 118:17, I shall not die but live to declare Your works.

As I rely solely upon You, Lord, according to 3 John 2, I declare that above all things I am prosperous and healthy, and therefore I speak divine healing over my cardiovascular system, neurological system, pulmonary system, gastrointestinal system, endocrine system, musculoskeletal system, dermatological system, psychological system, immune system, reproductive system, renal system, and hematological system.

According to Luke 13:11 and Psalm 138:8, I decree and declare that I am loosed from every infirmity, including deforming rheumatoid arthritis, degenerative osteo-arthritis, osteoporosis, spine compression, fractures, slipped or herniated disks, and chronic neck and back pain—and that I am free to move freely in order to fulfill God's original purpose for my life.

You have given me dominion and power over the enemy, and nothing shall by any means hurt me; therefore, according to Genesis 1:28 and Luke 10:19, I speak divine deliverance from every addiction to nicotine, alcohol, cocaine, heroin, hallucinogens, and any other form of drug addictions. I speak healing from chronic fatigue, chronic depression, chronic pain, overeating, excessive drinking, and inappropriate sexual activity.

**Father, in the name of Jesus, I decree and declare:**

That my spirit man is clad with the armor of the Lord and the armor of light.

That Your kingdom is my priority and Your assignment is my pleasure. Let Your kingdom come and Your will be done on the earth as it is in heaven.

I function and conduct my life's affairs according to Your original plan and purpose for me.

I walk in Your timing.

You are the one and true God, who makes everything work together and who works all things for good through Your most excellent harmonies. Cause my will to work in perfect harmony with Yours.

Evil shall not come near my dwelling, since I dwell in the secret place of the Most High God and dwell under the shadow of the Almighty.

I cause demonic, destiny-altering activities to cease. I take hold of the ends of the earth and shake evil out of its place.

I break evil and inappropriate thought patterns in my mind.

I speak peace into my life, relationships, ministry, workplace, and business.

Everything that is misaligned I command to come into divine alignment.

I have the mind of Christ and therefore seek things above and not beneath.

I ascend into new realms of power and authority and access new dimensions of divine revelation.

I will not backslide or look back into old ways, old methodologies, or old strategies unless directed by You to do so.

I wear the helmet of salvation to protect my mind from negative thoughts that would derail Your purposes and plans for me.

Truth protects my integrity, righteousness protects my reputation, the gospel of peace guides my every step, the shield of faith secures my future and destiny, and the sword of the Spirit grants me dominion and authority.

I decree and declare a prophetic upgrading of my thought life. I cancel the affect of negative, self-defeating thought processes and patterns and put them under my feet.

I possess a kingdom paradigm, which grants me new ways of thinking, new ways of working, and new ways of living.

New cycles of victory, success, and prosperity will replace old cycles of failure, poverty, and death in my life.

I now have a new, refreshed, cutting-edge kingdom mentality.

At Your Word, as a kingdom trailblazer, I pioneer new territory.

Everything that pertains to my life and godliness and everything prepared for me before the foundation of the world must be released in its correct time and season. I command everything to be released in Jesus's name.

I declare that there will be no substitutes, no holdups, no setbacks, and no delays.

Since Your Word is a lamp unto my feet and a light unto my path, I shall neither stumble nor fall.

I am excited; my spirit is ignited; I walk in favor with God and man.

I am a success-oriented individual, and everything I touch turns to "prophetic gold."

I am a successful business owner—an entrepreneur who provides good jobs to others.

Today I am blessed, there is no lack, all my needs are met, I am out of debt, and I have more than enough to give over and above all my needs.

All financial doors are opened, and all financial channels are free. Endless bounty comes to me.

Sufficient is Your provision for today.

I am healed and Spirit filled; sickness and disease are far from me.

I have buying power on my dollar, and I live in prosperity.

I confess that I only progress; I experience no setbacks and live a life filled with success.

I will persist until I succeed.

I walk in dominion and authority. My life is characterized by liberty.

There is no slackness in my hand. Where I stand, God gives me the land.

The blessings of the Lord make me rich, and I am daily loaded with benefits.

I am living my most blessed and best days now.

I am crowned with God's love and mercy. With all good things He satisfies me.

My home is a haven of peace.

I do my work as unto the Lord with diligence and in the spirit of excellence.

My home, business, departments, and ministries function smoothly and efficiently.

The Lord gives me wisdom, knowledge, and understanding as to how to do my work more effectively, professionally, and accurately.

The Lord gives me all the right people to work with and for me. Together we work as unto the Lord.

Relationships will come to me that are assigned to enhance my life and ministry for this season.

I call forth every individual and resource assigned to assist me in the fulfillment of my kingdom assignment during this season.

I attract only the things, thoughts, people, and resources suitable to undergird and facilitate God's original plan and purpose for my life.

I am favored by all who know me, meet me, work with me, and have any kind of formal or informal relationship with me.

I will work with You as my partner. I work according to Your daily agenda and perform for an audience of one—the Lord Jesus Christ.

My work is my worship.

You are teaching me how to improve my productivity—to work smarter and more efficiently.

I always function with an outstanding attitude and produce superior work.

You empower me to make positive and significant deposits in other people's lives.

I seek divine opportunities and occasions to help others succeed.

I maximize my potential and move boldly toward my destiny.

I am a purpose-driven, kingdom-principled, success-oriented individual, and I refuse to be distracted by insignificant things and people.

Let favor, well wishes, ambassadorial courtesies, kindness, and support be extended to me by all who are assigned to me, meet me, know me, and interact with me.

I do not procrastinate. I act now, without hesitation, anxiety, or fear.

I excel in all things, at all times, with all people, under every circumstance.

I will judge nothing and no one prematurely. I celebrate Your creativity in the diversity of ethnicities, nationalities, and humanity.

I am fruitful.

I have power to gain wealth.

Wherever I go, systems, institutions, cultures, environments, legislation, codes, ordinances, regulations, and policies adjust to accommodate my divine purpose.

I am adaptable and flexible and make needed adjustments.

I am in the perfect place for You to bless me.

My relationships are fruitful and mutually beneficial.

I am celebrated and loved by all who come in contact with me.

Everything about me is changing for the best.

I am healthy and physically fit.

Sickness and disease are far from me.

My mind is fortified and resolute.

My emotions are sound and stable.

My faith is steadfast and unfaltering.

The zeal of the Lord fills my soul and spirit.

Let there be no demonic encroachment. Let there be no satanic squatters—in the name of Jesus, get off my property, get off my territory, get out of my sphere of influence, get out of my family, get out of my relationships, get out of my finances, get out of my body, and get out of my mind.

I command mountains to be removed and to be cast into the sea.

I am gaining new territories: new emotional territory, new intellectual territory, new business territory, new spiritual territory, new ministerial territory, and new financial territory.

> *Father, I wait to see Your finished product. I look forward to the day that I will be transformed into the image of Your dear Son. My heart's deepest desire is to be like Him.*

*I seal these declarations in the name of Jesus, my Lord and Savior. Now unto Him that is able to do exceeding abundantly above all that I could ask or imagine, according to the power that works in me; to Him that is able to keep me from falling, and to present me faultless before the presence of His glory with exceeding joy, and to sustain my body, soul, and spirit; to the almighty God my heavenly Father, the King eternal, immortal, invisible—the only wise God—be honor and glory forever and ever. [Spend a few moments in praise and thanksgiving knowing that God has heard and will respond.] Hallelujah! I praise You, God. Amen!*

**"And so we have the prophetic word confirmed, which you do well to heed as a light that shines in a dark place, until the day dawns and the morning star rises in your hearts"**
**(2 Pet. 1:19).**

# THE ESSENCE OF A NEW DAY

This is the beginning of a new day
You have been given this day to use as you will.
You can waste it or use it for good.
What you do today is important
Because you are exchanging a day of your life for it.
When tomorrow comes, this day will be gone
  forever.
In its place is something that you have left
  behind…
Let it be something good.

—Author Unknown

# NOTES

## Introduction

1. Quoteopia.com, "Karen Ravn Quotes," http://www
.quoteopia.com/famous.php?quotesby=karenravn
(accessed June 6, 2007).

## Chapter One
## The Secret Is Out

1. University of Massachusetts–Amherst, "United States
Story Cycles: Charles W. Chesnutt," http://people
.umass.edu/engl480h/resources/chesnutt.html
(accessed June 6, 2007).

2. Wikipedia.org, s.v. "Dave Thomas (American
businessman)," http://en.wikipedia.org/wiki/Dave
_Thomas_(American_businessman) (accessed June 6,
2007).

## Chapter Two
## Mind Your Own Business

1. Wikiquote.org, "Marcus Aurelius: *The Meditations*,
4.3," http://en.wikiquote.org/wiki/Marcus_Aurelius
(accessed June 6, 2007).

2. James Allen, *As a Man Thinketh* (New York: Cosimo,
Inc., 2005), 26.

3. Cybernation.com, "Johann Gottfried Von Herder: Inspiration," http://www.cybernation.com/ quotationcenter/quoteshow.php?type=author&id=4126 (accessed June 6, 2007).

4. "Quincy Jones Interview: Music Impresario: the Quintessential Artist," interviewed by the Academy of Achievement, June 3, 1995, in Williamsburg, VA, and October 28, 2000 in London, England, http://www .achievement.org/autodoc/page/jon0int-1 (accessed June 21, 2007).

5. Lana K. Wilson-Combs, "Quincy Jones: His Honors Abound," *The Examiner*, posted on Examiner.com on January 25, 2007, http://www.examiner.com/ a-527824~Quincy_Jones__His_honors_abound.html (accessed June 6, 2007).

6. Encarta.MSN.com, s.v. "George Washington Carver," http://encarta.msn.com/encyclopedia_761574196/ George_Washington_Carver.html (accessed June 6, 2007).

7. "What Life Means to Einstein: An Interview by George Sylvester Viereck," *The Saturday Evening Post*, October 26, 1929, as quoted in Encarta.MSN .com, "Quotations From Encarta: Imagination," http://encarta.msn.com/quote_561559592/ Imagination_I_am_enough_of_an_artist_to_draw_ freely_upon_my.html (accessed June 6, 2007).

8. NobelPrize.org, "The Nobel Prize in Physics 1921," http://nobelprize.org/nobel_prizes/physics/ laureates/1921/ (accessed June 6, 2007).

9. JustDisney.com, "Walt Disney, Biography," http://www
   .justdisney.com/WaltDisney100/biography01.html
   (accessed June 6, 2007).

10. Allen, *As a Man Thinketh*, 49.

11. Dell.com, "Michael S. Dell: Chairman of the Board
    and Chief Executive Officer," http://www.dell.com/
    content/topics/global.aspx/corp/biographies/en/msd_
    index?c=us&l=en&s=corp (accessed June 6, 2007); also,
    Wikipedia.org, s.v. "Michael Dell," http://en.wikipedia
    .org/wiki/Michael_Dell (accessed June 6, 2007).

12. QuotesandPoems.com, "Hope and Dreams," http://
    www.quotesandpoem.com/quotes/showquotes/subject/
    Hope_&_Dreams/2373 (accessed June 6, 2007).

13. Wikipedia.org, s.v. "Coca-Cola," http://en.wikipedia
    .org/wiki/Coca-Cola (accessed June 7, 2007).

14. Wikipedia.org, s.v. "Bill Gates," http://en.wikipedia.org/
    wiki/Bill_Gates (accessed June 7, 2007).

15. Chicken Soup for the Mind, Heart and Soul, http://
    www.munic.state.ct.us/burlington/chicken_soup/
    chicken_soup_quotes_for_mind_heart_and_soul.htm
    (accessed June 21, 2007).

16. Bartleby.com, *Respectfully Quoted: A Dictionary of
    Quotations* (1989), s.v. "Daniel Hudson Burnham," no.
    1360, http://www.bartleby.com/73/1360.html (accessed
    June 25, 2007).

## Chapter Three
## The Creative Power of Spoken Words

1. QuotesandPoems.com, "Quotes by Author: Theodore
   White," http://www.quotesandpoem.com/quotes/
   listquotes/author/theodore_white (accessed June 7, 2007).

2. Quoteland.com, "Motivational," http://www.quoteland .com/author.asp?AUTHOR_ID=1347 (accessed June 25, 2007).

**Chapter Four**
**What Have You Put in the Atmosphere?**
1. Brainyquote.com, "Joel Osteen Quotes," http://www .brainyquote.com/quotes/quotes/j/joelosteen282005 .html (accessed June 25, 2007).

**Chapter Five**
**You Can Change the Course of Your Destiny**
1. Allen, *As a Man Thinketh*, 12.
2. Jennifer Kennedy Dean, *Live a Praying Life* (Birmingham, AL: New Hope Publishers, 2006), 59.
3. As quoted in Germaine Copeland, "Too Busy to Pray," March 2003, Prayers.org, http://www.prayers.org/ articles/article_mar03.asp (accessed June 7, 2007).

**Chapter Six**
**The Importance of Ordering Your Day**
1. Benjamin Franklin, *Poor Richard's Almanack*, Modern Library Paperback edition (New York: Random House, 2000), 83.
2. Ibid.

## Chapter Seven
## How to Become an Overnight Success

1. QuotesandPoems.com, "Quotes by Author: William James," http://www.quotesandpoem.com/quotes/showquotes/author/william_james/12749 (accessed June 8, 2007).

## Chapter Eight
## Commanding Your Morning

1. Walt Whitman, "Leaves of Grass," Book XI, as quoted at KnowledgeRush.com, http://www.knowledgerush.com/paginated/lvgrs10/lvgrs10_s12_p6_pages.html (accessed June 8, 2007).

# Know the
# Rules...Enemy...TRUTH

Know the Rules...
Know the Enemy...
Know the TRUTH!

There is a spiritual battle going on. In *The Rules of Engagement* prayer warrior and intercessor Cindy Trimm gives you the manual you need to wage effective warfare.

Using the authority you have been given by God, you can enter the realm of prayer-power where strongholds of the enemy are shattered and your true authority as a believer is unleashed.

It's time to beat the devil at his own game!

ISBN: 978-1-59979-340-5/$14.99

**To view these and other titles by Cindy Trimm, visit your local bookstore today.**

Charisma
HOUSE
A STRANG COMPANY

7325

# FREE NEWSLETTERS
## TO HELP EMPOWER YOUR LIFE

## Why subscribe today?

☐ **DELIVERED DIRECTLY TO YOU.** All you have to do is open your inbox and read.

☐ **EXCLUSIVE CONTENT.** We cover the news overlooked by the mainstream press.

☐ **STAY CURRENT.** Find the latest court rulings, revivals, and cultural trends.

☐ **UPDATE OTHERS.** Easy to forward to friends and family with the click of your mouse.

**CHOOSE THE E-NEWSLETTER THAT INTERESTS YOU MOST:**

- Christian news
- Daily devotionals
- Spiritual empowerment
- And much, much more

SIGN UP AT: **http://freenewsletters.charismamag.com**

6178